Prophetic Events Impacting This 1948 Generation

Prophetic Events Impacting This 1948 Generation

by Daniel Ropp

WESTBOW PRESS

A DIVISION OF THOMAS NELSON
& ZONDERVAN

WestBow Press books may be ordered through booksellers or by contacting:

WestBow Press
A Division of Thomas Nelson & Zondervan
1663 Liberty Drive
Bloomington, IN 47403
www.westbowpress.com
1 (866) 928-1240

ISBN: 978-1-5127-2228-4 (sc)

Library of Congress Control Number: 2015920122

Print information available on the last page.

WestBow Press rev. date: 12/4/2015

Table of Contents

Table of Contents Continued

Introduction

This book is intended to reveal some of the mystery of Bible prophecy much of which applies to this 1948 generation. There seems to be a growing amount of misinformation with regard to end time prophecy. What one believes will affect their understanding so we need to examine the evidence.

The angel in Revelation 19.10 said that the testimony of Jesus is the spirit of prophecy. You would think that the prophetic theme would be a priority in the Church in the end time, but in so many churches this is not the case. The theme of the Bible centers around Jesus so it only makes sense that we should be focusing on Him and His coming Kingdom, especially now, since this is the generation that ushers in the return of our Lord.

Yes, our generation is a unique generation from all others, and it is through Bible prophecy that we know about it. Our Lord is very gracious to inform us through His word that there is a flood event on the horizon, a flood of evil that will pervade society. There will also be an ark of safety event that will precede it by way of the catching out of the Church. Hopefully we will see the need to take the prophetic entreaties seriously.

The scriptures quoted are from the New King James Version unless otherwise noted.

Chapter One
The End Time

We use those words almost without giving them a second thought. So if someone was to come up and ask, "How do you know we are living in the end time" what would we say? Unbelievers typically believe that things will continue on in the usual way, but down inside they are somewhat challenged to believe this. Why? Because the events they see happening around them and around the world aren't so ordinary anymore. The events would be more truthfully described as unusual, record breaking or extraordinary. Also within our country we now have a president who has no qualms about disregarding our Constitution by using his executive orders, downsizing our military and purging it of anything Christian that he can. Free speech is now being replaced with political correctness. Yes, we would have to say he gave us change but that change is not normal it is abnormal. The outcomes we see are not favorable when they take away from us the liberties that we had in the past. The promise of better times are really not there for the unbeliever.

The Christian who understands Bible prophecy would say these things are to be expected because we are living in the end time. Christians have available to them insight into the end of the age from the writings of the prophets, from Jesus and the apostles, the early

Church fathers, and the Holy Spirit who will tell us things to come (John 16.13). Just by using the time frame given to us from the Bible we know human life began on this planet a little over 6,000 years ago. Some might be surprised as to what the early Church fathers believed in this regard. Irenaeus was one of them who lived 120-202 A.D. He said, "For in as many days as this world was made in so many thousand years shall it be concluded. For the day of the Lord is as a thousand years; and in six days created things were completed: it is evident therefore, that they will come to an end at the sixth thousandth year." [From Irenaeus chap. XXVII book V]

What he surmised was not a prophetic word from the Lord but this is what he believed. What is interesting is that the generation we are now living in is the period of the end Irenaeus spoke of, so he would say we are living in the end time. Irenaeus goes on to describe what society would be like in the end time. He said that people will be spiritually blind, not acknowledging the truth, in the depths of ignorance and as wastewater from a sink. Then he makes a crowning statement, "…And therefore, when in the end the Church shall be suddenly caught up from this, it is said, "there shall be tribulation such as not been since the beginning, neither shall be." [Irenaeus chap. XXIX book V]

So we will let Irenaeus be a documented witness that we are living in the time of the end. I mentioned previously several sources that would let us know we are living in the end time but there is another I didn't mention - **God's providence**. God is very much involved in the affairs of mankind, and I believe it would be accurate to say He is the chief of the selection committee. He selects which people are going to be at the head of governments, whether a country has rain or drought, even the names of people before they are born who will play a pivotal role in His redemption plan as well as the time of their births among other things.

Because of hindsight we can see now where God gave a very specific clue as **to when the end time generation would commence**. The clue He linked to Israel who would become His time clock for the rest of the world. But prior to that, the first clue to us began with the birth of Abram and he would become the father of the Hebrew people. So what was the clue? It was the year of his birth precisely 1948 years after Adam. One might think - ah, but that is just a coincidence. But was it really? Notice what God said about Himself in Isaiah 46.9b-10a. "...I am God and there is none like Me declaring the end from the beginning..." In this case, the beginning plan for the nation of Israel began with the birth of Abram. The next confirming clue God gave with Abram's grandson, Jacob who would later be called Israel from which the nation would be named. So what was the clue?

The clue was provided in a mystery when Jacob was 84 years old. This is when Jacob married Rachael

3

and the secret was in the meaning of their names once they were united. You see Jacob's name means "following after" and Rachael's name means "a lamb." Linked together it says, "following after, a lamb."

It isn't obvious, but 1948 years after Jacob married Rachael Jesus was born and John the Baptist declared Him to be the Lamb of God who takes away the sin of the world. This isn't the last time we see this remarkable time period of 1948 years given. During Jesus' ministry He gave us the parable of the fig tree. The fig tree in scripture represents the state of Israel. So the parable indicated that when the fig tree (Israel) emerged from its dormant state, (this implied it would be recognized again as the state of Israel), it would signal the time period of the last generation in which Jesus would return to earth and set up His kingdom to rule upon the earth for 1,000 years. The first part of this parable has been fulfilled when Israel was declared an independent state May 14, **1948**. Jesus also said it would be summer when it happened and the month of May is when summer starts in Israel and their independence was also declared on the very day of the Festival of the Fig Tree. Even the details of His prophecy were fulfilled.

Jesus went on to speak about the events that would take place in the 1948 generation. Many of us are familiar with those events Jesus spoke about and have observed them being fulfilled just like He said with the exception of the seven year tribulation and Jesus' return. But now Jesus goes on record

4

with a crowning statement in Matthew 24.34. As if it couldn't be anymore clear, He said, "Assuredly, I say to you this generation will by no means pass away til all these things take place." So Jesus is saying **this generation** will see the consummation of all these things. Yes, Jesus is affirming that those living in this 1948 generation are living in the end time! What follows the consummation of the age in the end time? Answer - a new age dawns where Jesus Christ will reign for 1,000 years on this earth with His saints. Yes, Jesus will soon be visibly present reigning as King over the whole earth. The prophet Hosea, who lived about 785 B.C., spoke of this. In Hosea 6.1-2 speaking about Israel he says, "Come and let us return to the Lord; for He has torn, but He will heal us; He has stricken but He will bind us up. After two days He will revive us; on the third day He will raise us up that we may live in His sight." In decoding his prophecy you realize that each of these days represents a thousand years. So part of his prophecy has been fulfilled where it says, "after two days He will revive us." With regard to this prophecy, when was Israel "torn" and "stricken?" It was in 63 B.C. when the Romans came into Israel and conquered it. That was the starting point for this prophecy. And when was Israel revived? They were revived in 1948 A.D. when they emerged from a dormant state after 2,000 years. The prophecy said it would be after two days or two thousand years. Was it? Yes, it was 11 years after! So this part of the prophecy has been fulfilled in our 1948 generation.

You see, in this prophecy the promise is made to the generation of Israel, now revived, that they will "live in His sight" on the third day. The second prophetic day has passed and the third day has begun. Yes, this 1948 generation has extended right into the third day and it is the generation that will visibly see Jesus return as King to the earth after which Israel is promised a spiritual restoration.

Yes, we can document that Hosea identifies the 1948 generation as the end time generation. From the evidence that we have, it is apparent that the destiny of many hang on whether one believes in the fulfillment of Bible prophecy or not. Bible prophecy, for the end time, does not end here as we will see in the next chapter. The evidence only becomes more compelling.

Chapter Two
God Has Not Compromised His Plan

God knows exactly what He is doing. Satan and the secular world do not want to believe they have lost their war against God. So the battles for the souls of men continue. In some respects it would seem that Satan has the upper hand. Most of the secular learning institutions exclude God from the learning process any way they can. Don't think that's true? Try teaching Creation Science in the classroom and see what happens. Try teaching that abortion is wrong and see what happens. I think I've made my point without needing to make a long list.

So what we have in society now is an on-going downward trend away from the things of God. In fact this trend would become so significant that it was prophesied in the Bible to happen in the latter days.

In the book of 1Timothy chapter four and verses 1-2 it says, "Now the Spirit expressly says that in latter times some will depart from the faith, giving heed to deceiving spirits and doctrines of demons speaking lies in hypocrisy, having their own conscience seared with a hot iron."

In the book of 2Timothy 3.1-4 it says, "But know this that in the last days perilous times will come: for men will be lovers of themselves, lovers of money, boasters, proud, blasphemers, disobedient to parents, unthankful, unholy, unloving, unforgiving, slanderers, without self control, brutal, despisers of good, traitors, headstrong, haughty, lovers of pleasure rather than lovers of God. This describes our present day society to a T. Therefore, we must indeed be living in the last days prophetic time period. So none of this has caught God by surprise. It was prophesied in His Word around 1900 years ago. These signs are a final warning of what is yet to come soon,

What emerges on the world scene in such a time as this is the antichrist. The Muslims call him their Mahdi and the apostle Paul identifies him as the man of sin.

Notice the following prophecy in the book of 2Thessalonians 2.9-12. It reads, "The coming of the lawless one is according to the working of Satan with all power, signs, and lying wonders, and with all unrighteous deception among those who perish, because they did not receive the love of the truth, that they might be saved. And for this reason God will send them strong delusion that they should believe the lie, that they all may be condemned who did not believe the truth but had pleasure in unrighteousness."

Yes, the antichrist will emerge to rule the world during the great tribulation time and Jesus identified that this would occur in the generation in which Israel would become an independent state once again. In Matthew 24.34 He said, "…this generation will by no means pass away til all these things take place." Jesus listed a number of things that would take place (Matthew 24.15-30) **in this generation**, and two very significant events were the great tribulation and His coming back to earth in power and great glory. What should get our attention is that over 67 years of this generation have already gone by!

In Matthew 24.37-39, Jesus also prophesied to say, "But as the days of Noah were so also will the coming of the Son of Man be. For as in the days before the flood, they were eating and drinking, marrying and giving in marriage, until the day that Noah entered the ark, and did not know until the flood came and took them all away, so also will the coming of the Son of Man be."

So how was it in the days of Noah before the flood? Well the people in Noah's day did not believe Noah's message of warning was relevant to them so they dismissed it out of hand. Wouldn't you agree the same thing is happening today fulfilling Jesus' prophecy?

The man of sin is about to emerge on the world stage and society has two choices; to align themselves with Christ or with the antichrist. Christ does not force anyone to accept Him as their Savior. He simply entreats you while the Age of Grace is still in your favor. The antichrist, on the other hand, will through his false prophet, force society to worship him. In Revelation 13.15-17 it says, "He was granted power to give breath to the image of the beast, that the image of the beast should both speak and cause as many as would not worship the image of the beast to be killed. He causes all, both small and great, rich and poor, free and slave, to receive a mark on their right hand or on their foreheads, and that no one may buy or sell except one who has the mark or the name of the beast, or the number of his name."

If you are wondering how those are killed who don't comply it is through decapitation (Revelation 20.4) the very thing ISIS is doing now in the Middle East. ISIS is the Mahdi's people - the antichrist's people. Do you see the handwriting on the wall yet?

God is allowing this time of trial for the world because the world has largely rejected Him. But as in the days of Noah there was an ark of safety but one had to get into it to be safe. That ark today is Jesus Christ. If one repents of their sins and accepts Christ as their Savior and Lord he will be raptured out and escape the great horrible tribulation period. But if one hasn't made the all important decision there isn't much time left in which to make that choice.

Chapter Three
Understanding The Kingdom of God

In the book of Mark 1.14-15 it says, "...Jesus came into Galilee preaching the gospel of God, and saying, 'The time is fulfilled, and the kingdom of God is at hand; repent and believe in the gospel.'" So the message of the kingdom of God was a message for people to repent and turn to God. What accompanied this message was the power and authority to cast out demons and to heal the sick.

So a person entering into the kingdom of God enters into a new freedom having their sins forgiven and the benefit of that is knowing His righteousness, joy, and peace in the Holy Spirit (Romans 14.17).

Now let's look at how blind the Pharisees were when they asked Jesus about this. In Luke 17.20-21 it reads, "Now having been questioned by the Pharisees as to when the kingdom of God was coming, He answered them and said, 'The kingdom of God is not coming with signs to be observed; nor will they say, "Look here it is!" or, "There it is!" For behold, the kingdom of God is in your midst.'" The New King James Version says that the kingdom of God is within you, but the NASV says the kingdom of God is in your midst and is more accurately rendered as we will see.

It is understood that the King is in charge of His kingdom. Yes, Jesus was exercising the power and authority of His Kingship right in their midst yet they didn't realize what was happening. They didn't recognize that the kingdom of God was present in their day nor did they realize what they were opposing.

Jesus went on to say in the following verses that the days would come when He wouldn't be among them and terrible times would come after (vv.26-29). But He also indicated that before judgments will fall upon the world there will be an exception (vv.30-36). First in verse 34 He says, "I tell you on that night there will be two in one bed; one will be taken and the other will be left. (v.35) There will be two women grinding at the same place; one will be taken and the other will be left. (v.36) Two men will be in the field; one will be taken and the other will be left."

In Tyndale's version (1534 A.D.) he translated the verse to read "...one will be received and the other will be forsaken," in each case. This clearly reveals Jesus was referring to the translation of the saints and those forsaken would be left to face judgments that will likely bring death to many of them.

So an unbeliever should really ask themselves why would I not want to enter into the kingdom of God since it will turn out to be very unprofitable not to? Since this is the generation of the Lord's return no one can afford to miss this **appointed time**!

Chapter Four
Major Turning Points In Time

These major turning points are linked to God's larger plan. **The first major turning point** came when Adam and Eve sinned by disobeying God in the garden of Eden. Adamic sin was perpetuated from that point onward. In fact it became such a major problem that God had to destroy the world by a flood, and this became **the second major turning point** in man's history.

The third major turning point came when God confused the languages of the people at the tower of Babel. Genesis 10.25 says, "To Eber were born two sons; the name of one was Peleg for in his days the earth was divided..."

The fourth major turning point came when God decided to set aside a people for Himself through whom the nations would be blessed. It began with the birth of Abram 1948 years after Adam. In Genesis 22.18 God speaking to Abraham said, "In your seed all the nations of the earth shall be blessed, because you have obeyed My voice."

The fifth major turning point came with the birth of Jacob. In Genesis 28.13-14 God spoke to Jacob in a dream and said, "I am the Lord God of Abraham, your father and the God of Isaac; the land on which you lie I will give to you and your descendants. Also, your descendants shall be as the dust of the earth...and in you and in your seed all the families of the earth shall be blessed." A few years later God changed Jacob's name to Israel (Genesis 32.28). A few more years go by and God tells Israel to go to Egypt and He would make of him a great nation there (Genesis 46.2-4).

The sixth major turning point came when Israel departed Egypt under Moses. Exodus 12.40-41 reads, "Now the sojourn of the children of Israel who lived in Egypt was four hundred and thirty years - on that very same day - it came to pass that all the armies of the Lord went out from the land of Egypt." Then 40 years later they entered the land of promise and claimed it as the land of Israel.

The seventh major turning point came with the birth of king David. In 2Samuel 7.16 the following is said concerning the Davidic kingdom: "And your house and your kingdom shall be established forever before you. Your throne shall be established forever." This was important because for this to happen the Messiah would have to come through the line of David, which He did. Matthew 1.1 says, "The book of the genealogy of Jesus Christ, the Son of David, the son of Abraham."

The eighth major turning point came with the birth of Jesus Christ. Yes, He was born in the land that was promised to Abraham, Isaac and Jacob. He completed, by fulfilling the first phase of His coming in being the sinless sacrifice to redeem the fallen race. This was huge! He revealed His Deity by all the

14

miracles that He did. Even the prophecies that He made are being fulfilled to our present day.

The **ninth major turning point** came with the birth of the Church after Jesus ascended into heaven. This initiated evangelism to the entire world to build Christ's kingdom.

The **tenth major turning point** happened in May of 1948 when Israel became an independent state once again. The reason it is so significant, is Jesus indicated that when that happened, it signaled the generation that would conclude the age, and this same generation will embrace the next three major turning points.

The **eleventh major turning point** will be when the rapture of the Church occurs and remember it is to happen in this generation we are living in now!

The **twelfth major turning point** will happen six months later when the two witnesses come to Israel, and in 3 ½ years they have 144,000 converts added to Christ's kingdom.

The **thirteenth major turning point** will happen one month after the two witnesses come to Israel and the antichrist emerges on the international world scene and is given authority to rule over the nations and he will rule for seven tumultuous years.

The **fourteenth major turning point** will happen when Jesus returns with millions of His saints (yes, in this generation) to set up His earthly kingdom and He will rule the world for 1,000 years.

Here's the rub. The antichrist and all those supporting him will think they have totally triumphed over Jesus Christ's followers only to be greatly surprised in the end when they see Jesus returning to overthrow all rebellion against God. This begins the judgment of nations (Matt. 25.31-46). Now the tables are turned and all the unjust and evil will be purged from Christ's kingdom and thrown into the lake of fire. Yes, anyone who was an accessory to the antichrist's objectives in supporting eradication of just people **will be purged from His kingdom and thrown into the lake of fire!** If this isn't a sober thought I don't know what is. The human race has been warned by Jesus what He will do when He comes back as the King of Kings. He won't be a pansy or a pacifist. He will be a Leader of leaders, a Lord of lords! Yes, it is decision time.

Revelation 22.10-11 states, "...the time is at hand. He who is unjust, let him be unjust still; he who is filthy, let him be filthy still; he who is righteous, let him be righteous still; he who is holy, let him be holy still." Jesus is indicating that by the choice we make we will have to live with the consequences of that choice!

Chapter Five
God Has His Appointed Times

There are future events that have their appointed times **designated by God**. Isaiah 44.6-7 says, "Thus says the Lord, the King of Israel, and His Redeemer, the Lord of hosts; 'I am the First and I am the Last; besides Me there is no God. And who can proclaim as I do? Then let him declare it and set it in order for Me. Since I <u>appointed</u> the ancient people, <u>and the things that are coming and shall come</u>.'"

God makes it clear there are future events that have their appointed times or set times. God never says, oops I missed that one. No He is <u>always</u> right on time. An example from Exodus 12.40-41 reads, "Now the sojourn of the children of Israel who lived in Egypt was 430 years. And it came to pass at the end of the four hundred and thirty years - <u>on that very same day</u> - it came to pass that all the armies of the Lord went out from the land of Egypt."

Another example is found in Leviticus 23.4-5. It reads, "These are the feasts of the Lord, holy convocations which you shall proclaim at their <u>appointed</u> times. On the fourteenth day of the first month at twilight is the Lord's passover." So this appointed time was fulfilled when? Exactly on the day Jesus was crucified. Matthew 26.17-18 reads, "Now on the first day of the Feast of Unleavened Bread the disciples came to Jesus saying to Him, 'where do You want us to prepare for You to eat the Passover?' And He said, 'Go into the city to a certain man, and say to him, 'the Teacher says, My time is at hand; I will keep the Passover at your house with My disciples.'"

Did you notice what Jesus said? He said, "My time is at hand." Jesus was referring to the appointed time set by God previously that we read about in Leviticus. Yes, Jesus was the Passover sacrifice and He fulfilled it to the very day!

In the book of Daniel, Gabriel reveals to Daniel that there is an appointed time for the indignation i.e. God's wrath. Daniel 8.19 reads, "...Look I am making known to you what shall happen in the latter time of the indignation; for at the appointed time the end shall be."

It was also revealed to Daniel that the actions of the antichrist in the end time, against the Jews would come to an end. Daniel 8.31 and 35 says, "And forces shall be mustered by him, and they shall defile the sanctuary fortress; then they shall take away the daily sacrifice and place there the abomination of desolation. [v.35] And some of those of understanding shall fall, to refine them, purify them, and make them white until the time of the end; because it is still for the appointed time."

The prophet Habakkuk was frustrated and dismayed that the wicked were getting by with so much violence and there seemed to be no justice. The vision he had sounds so much like what ISIS is getting by with now. God speaks to Habakkuk in chapter two and verse three. He says, "For the vision is yet for an appointed time; but in the end it will speak, and it will not lie..." Then in chapter three verses 12 and 13 it reveals what happens at the appointed time. "You marched through the land in indignation; You trampled nations in anger. You went forth for the salvation of Your people, for salvation with Your anointed. You struck the head from the house of the wicked..." This is exactly what it is talking about in Revelation 19.14-15 when Jesus comes back with the armies of heaven at the end of the great tribulation time.

It needs to be pointed out that Pharaoh was a type of the antichrist. When dealing with Moses he was a deceiver and a liar. It is interesting that after God's people were delivered out of Egypt that God destroyed not only Pharaoh but the entire Egyptian army. And so it will be at the end of the age that the antichrist will be destroyed and his army by none other than Jesus Christ who previously delivered His people out of the world.

The rapture is yet another appointed time soon to be fulfilled. It is found in Exodus 23.15. It reads, "You shall keep the Feast of Unleavened Bread (you shall eat unleavened bread seven days, as I commanded you, at the time appointed in the month Abib, for in it you came out of Egypt; none shall appear before Me empty handed)."

In Deuteronomy 16.3 Moses repeats God's command by saying, "...seven days you shall eat unleavened bread with it, that is the bread of affliction (for you came out of Egypt in haste)…"

Did you notice the words "bread of affliction?" That word affliction in the Hebrew can also mean "tribulation." If you go back over 400 years to when the latest edition of the Geneva Bible was written it uses that exact word "tribulation." So concerning the Feast of Unleavened Bread we see two components that it is associated with - a time of trouble (tribulation), and a time period. According to verse three they were to eat the bread of tribulation to remember the day in which they came out. So calling this unleavened bread, the bread of tribulation, associates it then with the tribulation since it is also associated with the time period of seven days a type of the seven years of the tribulation period; but they were to remember that **they were delivered from it!**

We know keeping the Feast of Unleavened Bread represented the very moment of departure from Egypt, the land of bondage, a type of the world, therefore the fulfillment of this appointed time represents the departing of the children of God from the world through the rapture. But did you notice the last part of verse 15? It said, "…none shall appear before Me empty-handed."

Guess where the Church, the people of God, are taken at the time of the rapture? First Thessalonians 3.13 says, "so that He may establish your hearts blameless in holiness before our God and Father at the coming of our Lord Jesus Christ with all His saints." So we come into the presence of God just as it was expected under the Feast of Unleavened Bread in the Exodus account.

The fulfillment of the Feast of Unleavened Bread goes even further, as in the Exodus account none of God's people were to appear before Him empty-handed. The answer or fulfillment of this is found in Revelation 22.12. It says, "And behold I am coming quickly, and My reward is with Me, to give to everyone according to his work." We won't be empty-handed. We will have our rewards.

I believe this is the next appointed time on God's calendar! When the rapture occurs it will constitute the greatest deliverance in the history of mankind outside of the cross. God told Moses this was to be remembered forever. This appointed time will affect everyone of us one way or another. Are you ready for it?

Chapter Six
Further Evidence

I mentioned previously that several things were on God's appointed time schedule from Leviticus chapter 23. Two of those events were the Passover and the Feast of Unleavened Bread. The Feast of Unleavened Bread was to be kept for seven days not just the evening of the Passover, and it was observed at the departure of God's people from Egypt.

Having reviewed these things, we go to an interesting statement made by Jesus, Himself, at the time He kept the last Passover with His disciples. The words of Jesus are found in Luke 22.15-16. He said, "With fervent desire I have desired to eat this Passover with you before I suffer; for I say to you, I will no longer eat of it **until it is fulfilled in the kingdom of God.**"

It would be only a matter of a few hours and Jesus would be fulfilling His role as the Passover Sacrifice so what still needed to be fulfilled in the kingdom of God? Answer - it was the Feast of Unleavened Bread and it would be fulfilled where? Answer - in the kingdom of God!

We find in Daniel 7.13-14 that the time comes when Jesus is brought before the Father and the kingdom that was promised to Him is finally given to Him. Also in Revelation 11.15 after the sounding of the seventh trumpet we find the kingdom is given to Jesus in heaven.

So the fulfillment of the Feast of Unleavened Bread is finalized in heaven! This feast was directly associated with the departure of God's people and the fulfillment of that type places God's people in heaven because Jesus said that it would be fulfilled in the kingdom of God. We are talking about the on-going fulfillment of the feast because it was to last for seven days which is symbolical of seven years the saints will be in heaven before returning with Christ to rule and reign with Him.

The Bride of Christ cannot fulfill this without them being translated so again this shows there will be a rapture of the saints, the Church, the Bride of Christ. Was God's people departing from Egypt a normal departure or was it God assisted? Even Moses said to the people that they had been born on eagles wings (Exodus 19.4). Yes, the time of God's people, the Church at the rapture will definitely be God assisted, and very soon the time of **our** redemption draws near!

Chapter Seven
Sign And No Sign

It begins with a question the disciples asked Jesus in Matthew 24.3. They asked, "…What will be the sign of your coming…?" So Jesus answers their question according to how they asked it, that is, with a sign that will precede His coming, and shows this would occur after the tribulation.

We read His answer in verses 29-30. He said, "Immediately after the tribulation of those days the sun will be darkened, and the moon will not give its light; the stars will fall from heaven, and the powers of the heavens will be shaken. Then the sign of the Son of Man will appear in heaven, and then all the tribes of the earth will mourn, and they will see the Son of Man coming on the clouds of heaven with power and great glory." We are told, that at the time of this coming, the atmosphere will be dark. So what is the sign? Simply this, a bright light piercing the darkness which precedes Jesus' descent with His saints. Second Thessalonians 2.8 confirms this when Paul said that when Jesus comes back He will destroy the antichrist "…with the brightness of His coming."

Jesus went on, to give the disciples additional information as well, concerning **His coming that would not be preceded by any sign** in Matt. 24.37-44. In these verses Jesus is distinguishing His coming in a different way, i.e. a coming that will take people by surprise. Jesus went on to say, "But as the days of Noah were so also will the coming of the Son of Man be. For as in the days before the flood they were eating and drinking, marrying and giving in marriage, until the day that Noah entered the ark, and did not know until the flood came and took them all away, so also will the coming of the Son of Man be. Then two men will be in the field, one will be taken and the other left. Two women will be grinding at the mill: one will be taken and the other left."

The surprise element here depicts a pretrib rapture. Did you notice that the believer and unbeliever were openly working side by side here which would be very unlikely if this were the end of a tribulation event. Mass slaughter of tribulation saints is happening in the last 3 ½ years of the tribulation (Daniel 7.25) so any saints who want to continue living at that time would have gone underground into hiding. They wouldn't be holding down public jobs since the mark of the beast would prevent them from buying or selling. So these working openly are depicting a pretrib environment, one in which a pretrib rapture occurs.

Scripture abounds with clues to a coming translation of the saints. Consider an interesting find from Malachi 3.17. It reads, "They shall be mine, says the Lord of hosts. On the day that I make them My jewels. And I will spare them as a man spares his own son who serves him." Now compare the Hebrew phrase "on the day I make them My jewels" to the Greek from the Septuagint which says, "on the day that I make them My acquisition." The word "acquisition" means a rescuing or delivering from in the sense of [I've come to collect, gather or pick up]. That is an almost perfect description of a catching away or a rapture event.

Chapter Eight
How Long After The Rapture Until The Seven Year Tribulation Begins

This was a mystery until just recently, but to begin to answer this question one of the things we need to know is when is the Festival of Firstfruits? The Festival of Firstfruits was to be celebrated when God's people entered the promised land. When God's people enter heaven this will fulfill the type of the Firstfruits.

Leviticus 23.10-11 puts it this way, "...When you come into the land which I give to you, and reap its harvest, then you shall bring a sheaf of the firstfruits of your harvest to the priest. He shall wave the sheaf before the Lord, to be accepted on your behalf; <u>on the day after the Sabbath</u> the priest shall wave it." This tells us the Feast of Firstfruits then was to be celebrated on the first day of the week. But what month was it celebrated?

Joshua 4.19 tells us when God's people entered the promised land. It reads, "Now the people came up from the Jordan on the tenth day of the first month..." Well the first month is the month Abib which corresponds to our March/April. Joshua 5.10 goes on to say, "Now the children of Israel camped in Gilgal, and kept the Passover on the 14th day of the month..." So what followed the Passover (by God's command) was the Feast of Unleavened Bread and then the Feast of Firstfruits all kept in the same month.

To be more precise as to the day in the month Abib that the Feast of Firstfruits was celebrated we look at two verses in Leviticus 23.15-16. It reads, "And you shall count for yourselves the day after the Sabbath, from the day that you brought the sheaf of the wave offering: seven Sabbaths shall be completed. Count fifty days to the day after the seventh Sabbath; then you shall offer a new grain offering to the Lord." We know the 50 day period as Pentecost. This is celebrated in the month Sivan which corresponds to our May/June calendar depending on which year it falls in.

So if you count backwards from Pentecost 50 days you come to the month Abib and the day of the Feast of Firstfruits which is on the first day of the week. This is how we know Jesus rose on the day of the Feast of Firstfruits as every one of the gospels says that He rose on the first day of the week.

It is important to remember what the Lord Himself declared concerning the firstfruits in Leviticus 23.17. He said, "You shall bring from your dwellings two wave loaves...they are the firstfruits to the Lord." Why two? Because there is a Gentile and Jewish component to the firstfruits. Jesus previously made provision for the Gentiles when He said in John 10.16 "Other sheep I have which are not of this fold them also I must bring..." There is further evidence of this on the day of Pentecost when the disciples found themselves speaking in languages of the Gentiles signifying to the Gentiles that the door was open to them to be included in the Church.

The Church, <u>as the Body of Christ</u>, is declared to be the firstfruits, and the 144,000 Jews in Revelation 14.4 are also declared to be the firstfruits to God. This is the only harvest mentioned in the plural (Firstfruits).

In fulfilling the gathering of the harvest, the Church is taken up to the throne of God prior to the start of the tribulation and the 144,000 at the middle of the seven years of the tribulation. How do we know this is the midpoint of the tribulation for them? Because after they are taken up, the 144,000 are seen standing before the throne of God in Revelation chapter 14 and we also see an angel warning the inhabitants of the earth not to take the mark of the beast, and this mark was not required by the antichrist until the midpoint of the tribulation.

You see in chapter 13 it is only after the antichrist is given authority to rule for the final 42 months (3 ½ years) that the false prophet causes people to receive the mark (Rev.13.16). One more way we know is in chapter 12 of Revelation as soon as the man child (144,000) is caught up to God's throne the woman (religious Israel) flees into the wilderness where she is fed for the last 1260 days of the tribulation (Rev.12.6) which represents the last 3 ½ years of that time period.

We now have all the information we need to determine the time lapse after the Church is caught up. First of all, we know the 144,000 are raptured in the month Abib because that is when the Feast of Firstfruits is celebrated and the translation of the 144,000 brings about the **final fulfillment** for the Feast of Firstfruits. This puts the month Abib at the end of the first 3 ½ years. So if you count backwards 3 ½ years from the month Abib you come to the starting point for the seven year tribulation period which turns out to be the Jewish month "Bul." The month "Bul" falls within the Oct/Nov time period on the Gregorian calendar.

I wondered down through the years how long after the rapture of the Church before the antichrist would be revealed. Would it be a matter of days, weeks, months or what? Now we know. Since the rapture takes place in the month Abib we have a transition period from Abib to Bul. This represents a delay of about seven months. But the Lord is keeping a carefully guarded secret not to reveal the year this occurs.

Transition from one major event to another doesn't happen like turning on a light switch. For example, from the cross to Pentecost there was a 50 day waiting period. So what might be occurring during the seven month transition? There is a possibility that Israel may be winding down a war with her enemies because what usually happens when a war concludes is signing a peace treaty. Isn't that what we are seeing at the beginning of the seven year period with the antichrist confirming a covenant of peace with Israel for seven years?

Now let's see what we find when we try and verify these time periods. Well we calculated from the midpoint of the tribulation backwards. What do we find if we calculate forward from the midpoint of the seven years to the end of it? Counting forward 3 ½ years you arrive at the month Tishri. What is supposed to happen at the end of the seven years is the Feast of Ingathering which represents **the last of the good harvest**. The Feast of Ingathering occurs in the month Tishri. Exodus 23.16 and Leviticus 23.39 both describe the Feast of Ingathering as being in the month Tishri which falls with the Sept/Oct period on the Gregorian calendar.

So now we have a good ball park figure for the length of the transition period which is very comforting because it embraces a sooner departure for the Church than what we may have previously envisioned.

Chapter Nine
What Do You Do With Truth?

There have been some flagrant accusations made against Christianity that merit a response. These accusations are not new. Their purpose has been to keep people from knowing the truth. You may recognize some of these accusations: 1) the Bible has been corrupted and can't be relied upon; 2) Jesus never said the things the Bible says He said; 3) Jesus didn't die on the cross; 4) Jesus never rose from the dead; 5) Jesus didn't ascend into heaven.

Satan is wanting to annul these major tenets of Christianity through these accusations. So let's examine the first accusation that the Bible has been corrupted. To start with, the accuser has a real problem because he would only know it has been corrupted if he had an uncorrupted version to compare it to. The best argument the accuser has is merely an assumption for which he has no proof!

Now let's look at the Bible's declaration concerning itself. In Psalm 138.2 it says, "...For You have magnified Your word above all Your name." This implies the highest honor that can be given is given to the word of God! The prophet Isaiah said, "...the word of our God stands forever"(Isaiah 40.8). So here we have the Bible's declaration that it is the truth. A Bible scholar would respond by pointing out some things. First, the Bible was written over some 1500 years so most of the writers did not know each other personally and therefore they could not collude with each other what they were going to write. For example, king David lived a few centuries after Moses so he couldn't change Moses' historical account (had he even wanted to) without introducing a conflict of interest in the Pentateuch. This never happened.

Secondly, some of the earliest versions of the Bible were the Syriac Bible available in the first and second century, the Vulgate by 400 A.D., the Masoretic text by 500 A.D., and they could compare the old testament with the Septuagint written about 250 B.C. The Septuagint Bible was the Bible used by Jesus and the apostles because it so accurately pointed to Jesus as the Messiah and so accurately fulfilled events in His life. This upset the Jews who did not want to accept Jesus as the Messiah so that in the second century A.D. they undertook a revision of the Septuagint to change the wording so it wouldn't portray Christ as the Messiah. So then the Christians began using the Hebrew writings.

It's true that scholars wondered for centuries how accurate the Bible we had was. Then a remarkable thing happened in the 20th century with the discovery of the Dead Sea Scrolls. They predated our oldest versions by about 1,000 years. When they compared the Dead Sea Scrolls with versions we already had it was discovered there was very little difference between them - only a few very minor scribal errors which did not compromise any Biblical doctrine.

So the Holy Bible has been preserved with great accuracy. Those who want to continue the reliability debate only do so because they do not want to believe the facts as they really are.

The Bible is further confirmed through archaeological discoveries of the cities and towns mentioned in scripture as well as kings who ruled over nations and empires during Biblical times. In fact the documentation for this has been so extensive that it has posed real problems for the skeptics.

Consider the next accusation that Jesus never said the things the Bible says He said. First of all, you can't deny or change what was said because it has been documented for all to read. Secondly, these statements the Bible said He spoke were all said by the same central figure. Thirdly, no one else takes credit for the things Jesus said but Jesus, and all the eye witnesses of that time credit Jesus for making His statements. It was His teachings and His commandments and His miracles that formed a large following of disciples. His disciples would not have been willing to follow Him **or give up their very lives for Him if He had been a fraud**. Jesus, Himself did not deny the things that He said concerning His Deity and it got Him crucified. Jesus was not likely taking the rap for someone else and someone else is never named. When His disciples evangelized they never proclaimed the words of someone else - only the message of Jesus as Savior of the world. I would say the burden of proof rests on the accuser as to who said the words the Bible attributes to Jesus.

Let's consider the next accusation that Jesus never died on the cross. The main question I have for the accuser is, can you point to even one case where a person was crucified as Jesus was, having first been beaten with whips that ripped His back into shreds causing a massive amount of blood loss, and then have large spikes driven into His hands and feet causing even more blood loss and then have a soldier pierce His side with a spear draining the blood from His heart, and who could then be able to come down from the cross many hours later without having died?

Secondly, Pilot did not allow Jesus to be taken down from the cross without ascertaining from the Centurion that Jesus was indeed dead. Also those who clamored for His death would not have allowed anyone to take Him down from the cross unless they were assured Jesus was indeed dead. Again the burden of proof that Jesus didn't die rests with the accuser. Denying reality does not change historical fact!

Then there are the accusations that Jesus didn't rise from the dead or ascend into heaven. Both are included together here because both events had many eye witnesses. The first evidence that Jesus rose from the dead was the soldiers who were assigned to guard the tomb fled into the city to tell the chief priests what happened. So we need to ask why were they so fearful and emotional if nothing had happened? They were fearful because they saw the power of God in action in Jesus' resurrection and those soldiers were not about to challenge Him! **They fled!**

When the disciples were later in Jerusalem proclaiming that Jesus was alive and that it was He who healed the lame man it upset the chief priests who wanted to shut them up. The only way they could possibly do that would be to produce the dead body of Jesus but they couldn't because He had risen from the dead and they knew that!

Then there was the occasion when Jesus appeared to His disciples in the upper room when the doors were locked. They believed, after He showed them His hands and feet where they had been pierced by the nails that fastened Him to the cross. The apostle Paul said that more than 500 saw Him at one time (1Corinthians 15.6). At Bethany while Jesus was among His disciples He ascended right before their eyes into a cloud and into heaven (Luke 24.50-51).

There is more evidence to believe that Jesus is the real deal. The old testament proclaimed Jesus would come as a suffering Messiah and also later as a kingly Messiah. Well Jesus and only Jesus has fulfilled all those prophecies of Him coming as a suffering Messiah! Note some of those prophecies.

The prophet Daniel revealed the Messiah would be cut off but not for Himself (Daniel 9.26). The prophet David revealed He would be given gall and vinegar to drink (Psalm 69.21), that they would pierce His hands and His feet (Psalm 22.16), and that they would divide His garments and cast lots for His clothing (Psalm 22.18). The prophet Isaiah revealed He would be beaten (Isaiah 50.6 & 53.5) and that He would bear the iniquity of our sins (Isaiah 53.6). The prophet Zechariah revealed He would be betrayed for 30 pieces of silver (Zechariah 11.12). His resurrection was foretold in Psalm 16.10.

These prophecies in Isaiah were given about 790 years before they were fulfilled; those in Daniel 640 years before, and those in Zechariah 550 years before being fulfilled. But here's the thing - they were all fulfilled in the time of Jesus' ministry by Jesus! **No one else has been able to make that claim, and that** is very very significant! Furthermore, there are no other books that have prophesied the birth, the time and place of birth, the life and death and resurrection of an individual centuries before those events were to be fulfilled of someone other than Christ! Are you starting to see the significance of this One called Jesus yet?

One of the things that amazes me is how God works behind the scenes to bring about the fulfillment of His word. Consider that the prophet Micah foretold, 750 years before the birth of the Messiah, that He would be born in Bethlehem. That wouldn't necessarily be a big deal if Joseph and Mary were already living in Bethlehem, but they were not. They were living in Nazareth of Galilee and showed no interest in going to Bethlehem. But God moved on a Roman king to issue a decree for everyone to go register at their home of birth. This forced Joseph and Mary to make the trip from Nazareth to Bethlehem. If they had of been even one day late Jesus would have been born somewhere else, but they made it just in time. If the Roman decree had been issued too late Jesus would not have been born there either. The time and location of His birth was fulfilled with precision. This again shows how reliable Bible prophecy is!

So who is this God who works behind the scenes to fulfill His great plan? Well Abraham knew Him, so let's see how Abraham addressed God, and how God addressed Himself to Abraham. In Genesis 14.22 Abraham said to the king of Sodom, "…I have raised my hand to the Lord (Yehovah), God (Almighty), the Possessor of heaven and earth." So he addresses God as Yehovah and the Almighty.

When God addresses <u>Himself to Abraham</u> in Genesis 15.7, "He said to him, 'I am the Lord (Yehovah), who brought you out of Ur of the Chaldeans, to give you this land to inherit it.'" Then again, in Genesis 17.1 God addresses Abraham this way, "…I am Almighty God (Almighty); walk before Me and be blameless."

Last of all, in Genesis 17.3 it says, "Then Abram fell on his face, and God (Elohiym) talked with him…" So in this verse, God is also known to Abraham as Elohiym. Continuing in verses 7-8 God says, "And I will establish My covenant between Me and you and your descendants after you in their generations for an everlasting covenant to be God (Elohiym) to you and your descendants after you. Also I will give you and your descendants after you the land in which you are a stranger all the land of Canaan as an everlasting possession: and I will be their God" (Elohiym).

Abraham's descendants were to address God as Elohim and Yehovah. So the descendants of Abraham who recognize, and address God by these names reveal who the true heirs to the land are. Abraham never addressed God as Allah nor did God address Himself to Abraham as Allah. So Allah and Jehovah are not the same God.

Now that we have looked at how precise some of these prophecies have been about Jesus we should also consider some of Jesus' own prophecies and how they are impacting this 1948 generation.

In Luke's gospel chapter 21, Jesus prophesied that **"nation will arise against nation."** So far, in **this** generation over 70 wars have occurred just from 1948 and that would not count WWI or WWII.

In the same chapter Jesus prophesied that **"kingdom would rise against kingdom."** So far there have been over 145 conflicts just since 1948. Kingdom conflicts being defined where a new foundation of power is trying to be established through conflict.

Jesus also prophesied that there would be **great earthquakes** in various places. I define a great earthquake where there is a significant loss of human life. So far there have been over 74 such earthquakes from 1948 the have taken over 1,558,390 lives.

Jesus also prophesied that there would be **famines**. Since 1948 over 23,600,000 have died from famine.

Jesus prophesied that there would be **pestilences**. Since 1948 over 31 million have died from various pestilences. Twenty five million just from aids alone. As recently as 1967 two million died from small pox.

Jesus prophesied **many would be hated and killed for His name's sake**. Since 1948 we are told over 6.93 million have been martyred for Christ around the world.

So how big do the numbers have to be before you say these prophecies of Jesus have certainly been fulfilled in this generation? The point is, what Jesus said would happen in this generation has happened!

So now what do we do with knowing that Bible prophecy is 100% accurate. Since so much of it centers around God's great unfolding plan and the center of His plan centers around His Son Jesus then we need to understand what this all means.

Philippians 2.9-11 gives a brief summary of what is ahead. Speaking of Jesus; "...God also has highly exalted Him and given Him the name which is above every name, that at the name of Jesus every knee should bow of those in heaven, and of those on earth, and of those under the earth, and that every tongue should confess that Jesus Christ is Lord to the glory of God the Father." Can you think of anyone who these verses will offend? How about Satan for starters, and every other religious leader in the world who isn't a Christian, and those who presently reject Christianity period. This is one reason why so many nations are out to destroy Israel because their existence is a testimony to the fulfillment of Bible prophecy and unless they can change that they will have to admit the Bible is true; its prophecies being true, and that is the last thing they want to accept.

Chapter Ten
Shock And Awe

Is there anything more sad than those who are deceived and who are being deceived? For example, lifted up on the same pedestal are those who place, Judaism, Christianity, and Islam. There are supposed to be enough similarities between them that they should be able to live together in peace. Judaism and Islam are similar in that they both reject Christ as the Way and they both reject Christ's Deity. His Deity was proclaimed clearly by the prophet Isaiah. In Isaiah 7.14 it says, "Therefore the Lord Himself will give you a sign, 'Behold the virgin shall conceive and bear a Son and shall call His name Immanuel.'"

The name **Immanuel means God with us**. In Isaiah 9.6 it says, "For unto us a child is born, unto us a Son is given; and the government will be upon His shoulder. And His name will be called Wonderful, Counselor, **Mighty God...**" These prophecies concerning the Messiah Jesus were documented approximately 750 years before He came.

So how would His Deity be recognized if He was truly God in man? Expressing His Deity would be to do supernaturally what no other man could do. For example, He turned water into wine (John 2.2-11)

He cleansed lepers (Luke 17.12-14); restored a man's withered hand to be whole (Matthew 12.10-13); raised a widow's son from the dead (Luke 7.11-15); fed 5,000 people with only five loaves and two fish (Luke 9.13-17); gave sight to two blind men (Matthew 9.27-31); walked on the water of the sea of Galilee (Matthew 14.24-33) and there are many more miracles which can be cited, but surely one can see these miracles confirmed His Deity. The common people in His day were in awe that he could do these mighty miracles (Mark 6.2).

Those who reject Christ have a real problem and many may not even realize they have a problem. Their problem is defying truth. Truth is expressed in fulfilled Bible prophecy concerning Christ! Yes, many will continue to reject Christ not understanding the peril that awaits them in doing so. There are really two camps here.

The first are those who have convinced themselves that it doesn't matter what you believe. The second are those who hold to a religion that believes they are right and Christianity is wrong. So what's the problem? The problem is, both groups are even now facing the fact that all Bible prophecy concerning Christ is being fulfilled without any error! What do you do with 100% accuracy? Ignore it? Disbelieve it? or believe it?

Jesus commented on a question that was posed to Him. "Then one said to Him, Lord are there few who are saved? 'And He said to them, strive to enter through the narrow gate, for many I say to you, will seek to enter and will not be able'"(Luke 13.23-24). In Matthew 7.13-14 Jesus said, "Enter by the narrow gate;

for wide is the gate and broad is the way that leads to destruction, and there are many who go in by it. Because narrow is the gate and difficult is the way which leads to life, and there are few who find it."

Truth is actually alive in the person of Jesus Christ! The miracles that were performed at the hands of the apostles would not have happened if Jesus hadn't rose from the dead. Saul, the Christian hater, would not have been converted to Christianity if he hadn't had a personal encounter with Jesus Christ. The book of the Revelation of Jesus Christ would not have been written if Jesus hadn't rose from the dead. In Revelation 1.18 Jesus says, "I am He who lives, and was dead, and behold, I am alive forevermore."

Oh yes, the shock and awe is stated in Revelation 1.7. It says, "Behold, He is coming with clouds, and every eye will see Him, even they who pierced Him. And all the tribes of the earth will mourn because of Him. Even so. Amen."

Chapter Eleven
End of The Age - End of The World

There is a difference between the global events for "end of the age" and that of "end of the world." One thousand years separate these times from each other. Jesus mentions the end of the age in Matthew 13.39 when He says, "...the harvest is the end of the age."

In Matthew 13.38-42 Jesus is explaining the parable of the wheat and the tares. There were two harvests - that of the "first fruits" and the last of it called the "ingathering" at the end of the year, and is described in Exodus 23.16, but Jesus in the parable was focusing on the last of it.

He said, "The field is the world, the good seeds are the sons of the kingdom, but the tares are the sons of the wicked one. The enemy who sowed them is the devil, the harvest is the end of the age, and the reapers are the angels. Therefore, as the tares are gathered and burned in the fire, so it will be at the end of this age. The Son of Man will send out His angels, and they will gather out of His kingdom all things that offend, and those who practice lawlessness and will cast them into the furnace of fire. There will be wailing and gnashing of teeth."

So what Jesus is saying here is that when He begins His earthly reign He will first of all purge it of the unjust - those who were an offense, a stumbling block to any and all who were trying to enter into the kingdom of God as well as those who are lawless. This is also clearly emphasized from 2Thessalonians 1.6-10.

The apostle Paul was letting the Christians know their suffering for Christ was not in vain. He said, "Since it is a righteous thing with God to repay with tribulation those who trouble you and to give you who are troubled rest, with us, when the Lord Jesus is revealed from heaven with His mighty angels, in flaming fire taking vengeance on those who do not know God, and on those who do not obey the Gospel of our Lord Jesus Christ. These shall be punished with everlasting destruction from the presence of the Lord and from the glory of His power, when He comes in that day to be glorified in His saints..."

This clearly reveals when the end of the age is. What we see happening in the parable of the wheat and the tares is a separating of the just from the unjust. This is also known as the judgment of the nations. This is referenced in Matthew 25.31-32. Jesus said, "When the Son of Man comes in His glory, and all the holy angels with Him, then He will sit on the throne of His glory. And **all nations** will be gathered before Him, and He will separate them one from another, as a shepherd divides his sheep from the goats."

The picture that one needs to see here is that when a nation of people are brought before the Lord the angels separate out of that nation the just from the unjust. The just will go to the Lord's right hand and the unjust to His left hand til all are separated.

The just will be allowed to continue to live in Christ's kingdom but the unjust - well Jesus says it best in verse 41. "Then He will say to those on the left hand, 'Depart from Me, you cursed, into the everlasting fire prepared for the devil and his angels.'" This is a judgment that precedes the Great White Throne judgment by a thousand years.

If you remember from Matthew 13, those who will be purged out of Christ's kingdom are those who offend. Those who offend are those who prevent others from entering the kingdom of God as well as themselves. This is a serious charge, so would you agree that the following categories make the list of those who offend? 1)Those who teach that the Bible is not true; 2) Those who teach that you won't have to be accountable to God for your life; 3) Those who try to get you to deny Christ or be killed; 4) Those who just simply lawlessly kill Christians because they are Christians; 5) Those who forbid you to hear the Word of God; 6) Those who slander and defraud others; 7) Those who promote false religions and doctrines; 8) Those who would forbid to pray in the name of Jesus; 9) Those who would forbid the spread of the Gospel through missionaries in their country; 10) Those who promote an anti-God curriculum in the public schools and universities; 11) Those who suppress truth about God or the Bible where not doing so would confirm the truth. This list could be expanded, but you get the point.

It is amazing to me, that during the great tribulation time people will be subjected to severe judgments, and after all that they still do not repent of the murders, sorceries, sexual immorality or their thefts (Revelation 9.21). These judgments were intended for the purpose of putting pressure on people so they would repent and so God wouldn't have to send them to a devil's hell.

So this is what brings the end of the age to a close. The good news is that those who repent and turn from their sins now and commit to His Lordship will be caught up from this escaping the sentence of damnation.

Now we turn our attention to the subject of "the end" of the world. Jesus actually addresses it twice in **Matthew 24**. In verses 35-36 Jesus said, "Heaven and earth will pass away, but My words will by no means pass away. But of that day and hour no one knows, not even the angels of heaven, but My Father only."

It should be obvious from these verses that the 1,000 year reign of Christ will have concluded as well as the event of the Great White Throne judgment.

The first time Jesus spoke of "the end" it has fostered a great deal of misunderstanding. In verse 14 He said, "And this gospel of the kingdom will be preached in all the world as a witness to all the nations, and then the end will come."

Jesus was answering the disciples question from the way they asked it in verse three. In verse three they asked, "And what will be the sign of Your coming and of the end of the world." More recent translations use the word "age" in place of the word "world." I noticed the King James translation, the Geneva translation, and the Tyndale translation all use the word "world" and I believe that is the correct rendering.

The misunderstanding surrounding this verse goes farther than this. As an example, many have mis-read verse 14 to say, and this gospel of the kingdom will be preached in all the world as a witness to all the nations and then the rapture will come. The word rapture or the word translation is no where found in this verse. So we really don't have grounds to believe that Jesus was referring to the rapture here. Therefore, if we hold to the view that Jesus really is referring to the end of the world, as He was asked, it therefore implies, then that even during His millennial reign the Gospel will still go forth to the nations.

It will probably come as a surprise to some to discover the prophet Isaiah reveals that the Gospel will go forth even during the millennial reign of Christ. Isaiah 2.2-3 says, "Now it shall come to pass in the latter days that the mountain of the LORD's house shall be established on the top of the mountains, and shall be exalted above the hills; and all nations shall flow to it. Many people will come and say, 'Come, and let us go up to the mountain of the Lord, to the house of God of Jacob; He will teach us His ways, and we shall walk in His paths.' For out of Zion shall go forth the law, **and the word of the LORD** from Jerusalem." From this verse we find it is Israel who will now pick up the baton, so to speak, and carry the responsibility of getting the Gospel to the ends of the earth. This is more clearly seen in Isaiah 49.3,6.

It reads, "and He said to me, you are **My servant O Israel** in whom I will be glorified. [v6] Indeed He says, 'It is too small a thing that you should be My servant to raise up the tribes of Jacob and to restore the preserved ones of Israel; **I will also give you as a light to the Gentiles**, that you should be My salvation **to the ends of the earth.**'"

This shows the world still needs the Gospel preached to them during the millennial reign of Christ. Isaiah further implies this in chapter 52 verses 7 and 10. It reads, "How beautiful upon the mountains are the feet of him who brings good news, who proclaims peace, who brings glad tidings of good things, **who proclaim salvation**, who says to Zion, your God reigns! [v.10] The Lord has made bare His holy arm in the eyes of all the nations; and all the ends of the earth shall see the salvation of our God."

Satan and his demons will be confined to the bottomless pit for the millennial reign of Christ so Satan won't be able to hinder the spread of the Gospel then. People will also have extended life spans allowing more time for the Gospel message to get to them. Yes, Jesus has indicated that by the end of the thousand years the whole world will have been reached.

It should be pointed out that "the end" here is not to be confused with the resurrection at the last day (John 11.24). The resurrection at the last day is simply the time of the resurrection of the righteous (Luke 14.14) and it signaled the end point for the Church dispensation. Once this translation of saints occurs no one else will get to be in the Bride of Christ - the door will be closed. Yes, there will be those who will be saved during the great tribulation time but they are a distinct category of saints narrowly defined as those saints who come out of the great tribulation.

We must not forget there was an **appointed time** for Christ's first coming, and He kept it, and there is an **appointed time** for His next coming for the Church <u>and He won't be late for it</u>. We know that His appointed time for the rapture will take place in our generation!

Chapter Twelve
Psalm 2.1-5 Warring Against God

The fulfillment of Psalm 2.1-5 is quickly approaching. It reads, "Why do the nations rage, and the people plot a vain thing? The kings of the earth set themselves, and the rulers take counsel together against the Lord and against His anointed saying, 'Let us break their bonds in pieces and cast away their cords from us.' He who sits in the heavens shall laugh; the Lord shall hold them in derision. Then He shall speak to them in <u>His wrath</u> and distress them in his deep displeasure."

This passage speaks to those who are enemies of God and of Jesus Christ. All those <u>who reject</u> the saving grace of Jesus are His enemies. To be a little more specific it would include the anti-God professors in our universities and those who support them; radical or fundamentalist Muslims; Satanists and all other religions that reject Christ as Savior and Lord. They think (in vain) that if they just get rid of all the Christians they won't have to be accountable to God. This is why ISIS is being so bold in the middle east to slaughter Christians. ISIS is beyond barbaric; they are demonic. They think their hour to succeed has come. But Satan has played his hand a little too soon. That authority has not been given to him until the last half of the great tribulation time (Daniel 7.25).

God has a payback time and it is called the time of His wrath (Psalm 2.5). I've been intrigued by just one little aspect of God's wrath as described in the 6th trumpet judgment in Revelation 9.15. We read, "So the four angels who had been prepared for the hour and day and month and year were released to kill a third of mankind."

One might think this verse is just simply implying that the final moment arrived where the four angels could now unleash this judgment. The words they "were released" imply that, but it doesn't explain the words "for the hour and day and month and year." Those words reveal that is how long the four angels had prepared for this judgment to last. This reveals the sixth trumpet judgment, all by itself, will last a little over 13 months and it will kill ⅓ of mankind in that time period.

The destroying army involved numbers 200 million (v.16), and the judgment includes destroying winds (Rev.7.1) which will likely be caused from nuclear explosions. Only one nation on earth has the funds and manpower to field an army of 200 million and that is Red China. This has never been possible in any prior generation. What do you do with tens of millions of young men that will never have a wife because of China's one child policy? You march them off to war to conquer nations. Since Communism doesn't believe in any God, China will come to believe they must stop this world's mad man, (the antichrist), a Muslim who now wants to be worshipped as God, and annihilate his followers. Do you realize how many people ⅓ of the earth's population is? That is over 2.3 billion people who are killed under this **one** judgment alone!!

The sixth trumpet judgment is initiated in the latter part of <u>the first half</u> of the great tribulation. We know this because the two witnesses are still on the earth during the sixth trumpet judgment, and their ministry was only to last for 3 ½ years. It is only <u>after</u> they are killed and resurrected that the 7ᵗʰ trumpet is sounded for more judgment.

Up until now the role of the 200 million man army has not been directed at the antichrist but has been to just conquer as many nations as possible in its quest to be world conquerer. But China halts their war of aggression after 13 months perhaps to allow for burying the dead and for resupplying their forces and take the time needed to re-evaluate their next course of action. One thing we aren't told is how many of their own forces were killed during this time. Later, we know from Revelation 16.12-14 and Daniel 11.44-45, that this formidable army moves again from the east to destroy the antichrist's army which culminates in the battle of Armageddon (Revelation 16.16).

I believe this is the time Jesus spoke of when He said, "And unless these days were shortened no flesh would be saved" (Matthew 24.21-22).

Chapter Thirteen
The Timing of Israel's Peace

Where do we get the idea of peace for Israel? It is derived from Daniel 9.27 and reads, "Then he shall confirm a covenant with many for one week..." The "he" here is understood to be the antichrist and the word "week" means a shubua or one seven and is understood to be for seven literal years. Since the antichrist is only in power for seven years, and since the great tribulation period is only seven years long, then we conclude that the antichrist confirms a covenant with Israel when he first comes on the world scene.

The fact that the scripture makes this a leading declaration it can mean only one thing - the Moslems want it as much as Israel. Why would the Moslems want it? I believe it is because Israel has soundly defeated them in another all out war. So the expected conclusion is to sign a covenant of peace and it is declared to be for seven years.

Some talk about the covenant of peace being broken after 3 ½ years but that isn't entirely true. What infuriates the antichrist is the offering of sacrifices at the temple, and he does put a stop to them and it compels the religious Jews to flee into the wilderness. But most of Israel is secular as are the Jews in the United States, and they don't want to have anything to do with Judaism.

In Daniel 11.30 we find the antichrist shows regard to those who forsake the holy covenant. So Israel, as a nation, is still at peace with their neighboring nations until nearing the end of the seven year period when the battle of Armageddon forces them to engage in war again.

At the middle of the seven years of the tribulation the severity of events greatly increases as though they weren't bad enough already. This last period is known as the Day of the Lord. In Malachi 4.5 the prophet describes the Day of the Lord by saying, "Behold I will send you Elijah the prophet before the coming of the great and dreadful day of the Lord." So it is described as a time that people will dread and not a time that people will look forward to.

The apostle Paul explains the "day of the Lord" very well in 1Thessalonians 5.2-3, 9. He said, "For you yourselves know perfectly that the day of the Lord so comes as a thief in the night. For when they say, 'Peace and safety!' then sudden destruction comes upon them as labor pains upon a pregnant woman. And they shall not escape. [v.9] For God did not appoint us to wrath, but to obtain salvation through our Lord Jesus Christ." A couple things stand out here. One, it is a time that brings sudden destruction from which people cannot escape and it also includes great calamity from God's wrath.

Paul makes another very good point from verses 4 and 5. He said, "But you brethren are not in darkness, so that this day should overtake you as a thief. You are all sons of light and sons of the day. We are not of the night nor of darkness."

When Paul says that we are sons of the day, he means sons of the day of Grace. Therefore, he contrasts the Day of Grace to the day of darkness where grace is not found.

The apostle Paul made a second attempt to clarify the sequence of events to the Thessalonians in 2Thessalonians 2.1-3. He said, "Now brethren, concerning the coming of our Lord Jesus Christ and our gathering together to Him, we ask you not to be soon shaken in mind or troubled, either by spirit or by word or by letter, as if from us, as though the day of the Lord had come. Let no one deceive you by any means; for that day will not come unless the falling away comes first and the man of sin is revealed, the son of perdition."

In verse two some translations read day of Christ instead of day of the Lord (and they aren't the same) and it has caused confusion in the way the verse is interpreted. We know the correct word is "Lord" by the reaction of the Thessalonians when Paul said to them not to be alarmed or shaken in mind or troubled.

There were some in the community that were saying that the day of the Lord had come which then left them to believe they had missed the coming of Christ for His saints. But Paul wanted to reassure them that the day of the Lord had <u>not</u> come either. Then he listed the events that had to take place before even the day of the Lord could come, namely a falling away, and the man of sin had to be revealed, none of which had occurred.

One needs to be aware that the apostasia or the falling away has now been fulfilled in our time.

It isn't something we are still waiting for. The apostasia had not happened yet at the time of the Thessalonians in Paul's day. That fact alone puts us another big step closer to the time of the rapture.

So what do we know about the falling away? In Asia minor the churches dwindled to where they were taken over by the Muslims and many of the churches were made into mosques. The Church attendance in Europe has fallen off dramatically to where very few attend anymore. In America church kids went off to college and were brainwashed into existentialism and so doubted their Biblical upbringing and their need to attend anymore. Now we have a society with a very liberal view point so much so that when they have to make a decision to choose between Biblical principles versus society's mores they choose society's philosophy because political correctness has become the absolute standard to live by rather than the Word of God.

Many of our Bible colleges have also completely closed. Even the Pentagon is trying to force our chaplains out of the military if they oppose homosexuals and gay marriage. They are forbidden to pray in the name of Jesus. As they can, the ten commandments are being removed from government property. Many public schools have banned the

Bible and prayer in the school. I could go on but it should be evident that we have seen the fulfillment of apostasia - the falling away. Yes, the rapture will occur first before the antichrist is revealed!

Chapter Fourteen
Understanding More of God's Ways

To understand how prophetic events will unfold one must consider God's thinking that goes into His great plan. For example, in John chapter five, Jesus was attempting to get His hearers to understand that **He was** the resurrection and the life, and then went on to say there would be two resurrections. Verses 28 and 29 read, "...the hour is coming in which all who are in the graves will hear His voice and come forth - those who have done good, to the resurrection of life, and those who have done evil, to the resurrection of condemnation."

So Jesus explains that there are two types of resurrections. One is to life and one is to condemnation. It is Revelation chapter 20 that reveals the resurrection to condemnation doesn't occur until a thousand years after the resurrection to life has been completed.

In addition, we discover something else when we read verses 4-5. It says, "...Then I saw the souls of those who had been beheaded for their witness to Jesus and for the word of God, who had not worshipped the beast, or his image, and had not received his mark on their foreheads or on their hands. And they lived and reigned with Christ for a thousand years. But the rest of the dead did not live again <u>until the thousand years were finished</u>. This is the first resurrection."

The only saints described in these verses are the great tribulation saints and yet they are declared to be in the first resurrection. Why is that? Because it is a resurrection unto life. It is verse six that reveals the first resurrection consists of parts. It reads, "Blessed and holy is he who has part in the first resurrection..."

When Jesus was resurrected it was to life; when the two witnesses are raised after three days it will be to life, and when the rapture occurs it will be a resurrection to life, and when the old testament saints are resurrected it will be to life. God considers all of these to be a part of the first resurrection - the resurrection to life.

Now to know precisely when the great tribulation saints are resurrected all we have to do is note where they follow in the sequence of events that is given to us. We observe this sequence beginning in chapter 19 and verse 14 where it shows the armies of heaven following Jesus to earth. It reads, "And the armies in heaven, clothed in fine linen, white and clean, followed Him on white horses." Verse 19 shows the impending battle will be waged against the earth's armies. It says, "And I saw the beast, the kings of the earth, and their armies, gathered together to make war against Him, who sat on the horse and against His army." Next the beast and the false prophet are cast alive into the lake of fire (v.20) followed by Satan being bound and cast into the bottomless pit (chapter 20 verses 2-3), followed by thrones of judgment being set up (v.4) and then the great tribulation saints are resurrected (v.4).

There is a particular group of saints that will be resurrected to life that are Daniel's people i.e. the old testament saints. Notice how Daniel 12.1-2 reads, "At that time Michael shall stand up, the great prince who stands watch over the sons of your people; and there shall be a time of trouble, such as never was since there was a nation, even to that time. And at that time your people shall be delivered, everyone who is found written in the book. And many of those who sleep in the dust of the earth shall awake, some to everlasting life..."

The description of the time of trouble here is referring to what is known as the time of Jacob's trouble and it commences half way through the great tribulation time. Jesus established when this would be in Matthew 24.14 & 21, and is confirmed in Daniel 9.27 to occur at this time. So we see the old testament saints are resurrected half way through the tribulation time.

I find it interesting that the Bride of Christ will be with Him before the old testament saints are resurrected. Is this related to Jesus' statement that the first shall be last and the last shall be first?

I also find an interesting link between the very first two prophecies of scripture and to note their relationship. In the first prophecy God was speaking to Satan, in Genesis 3.15, and said, "And I will put enmity between you and the woman, and between

62

your seed and her seed; He shall bruise your head…"
So in this first prophecy we see that the significant person here is Christ who will subdue Satan at some point in time.

The second prophecy in scripture was given by Enoch. Now Enoch, himself, is a type of the Bride of Christ. There are 365 days in a Gentile year and Enoch, a Gentile, lived 365 years and then was raptured. He was raptured because he had a relationship with God, for the scripture says he walked with God. Jesus' bride will have a relationship with Him and be fully dedicated to Him, and it is interesting that Enoch's name means dedication. Enoch was the seventh from Adam and seven is the number of completion. With regard to the Church, Colossians 2.10 says, "and you are complete in Him who is the Head of all principality and power."

Enoch's prophecy is not found in the old testament but in the book of Jude verses 14-15. It reads, "Now Enoch, the seventh from Adam, prophesied about these men also, saying, 'Behold the Lord comes with ten thousands of His saints to execute judgment on all, to convict all who are ungodly among them of all their ungodly deeds which they have committed in an ungodly way…"

So this second prophecy portrays the Bride of Christ as being with Jesus once you understand the prophecy. This reveals how much Jesus values His relationship with His Bride in that the second prophecy includes the presence of His Bride.

I'm sure you get the part that parallels the Revelation passage of the saints coming back with Jesus to wage war on the ungodly. But how many stop to think about how those saints got to be with Jesus in the first place before they came back with Him? Those saints that are coming back with Him (Rev.19) to conquer the ungodly enemies of Christ can't be great tribulation saints since those saints will not have been resurrected yet. Therefore, those saints who accompany Jesus at His return must be pre-tribulation saints, those who have been recipients of a pretrib rapture.

Verse 14 of Jude <u>doesn't</u> say Jesus is coming back with ten thousand saints but rather with ten thousands (in the plural) of them. That means multiplied ten thousands. Just ten thousand times ten thousand equals 100 million. The earth will then be faced with an impossibly huge heavenly army and the following words of Jesus will be fulfilled at that time. He said, "Then the sign of the Son of Man will appear in heaven, and then all the tribes of the earth will mourn, and they will see the Son of Man coming on the clouds of heaven with power and great glory" (Matthew 24.30).

I believe Jesus is in love with His Bride. When Jesus spoke of Father God He would call Him Theos, but when He spoke of Himself, He used the word Kurios. Now when Jesus quotes the greatest commandment, in Matthew 22.37, He said, "You shall love the Lord (Kurios) your God with all your heart, with all your soul, and with all your mind." So Jesus was referring to Himself when He was quoting this scripture and it showed relationship with Him was at the top of His list of what was important!

Can you see how God is thinking to fulfill His great plan?

Chapter Fifteen
Insight From Peter's Sermon

Peter was addressing a crowd that was marveling at the healing of the lame man, but Peter was attempting to focus the crowd's attention on Jesus. In Acts 3.18-21, 24 he said, "But those things which God foretold by the mouth of all His prophets that the Christ would suffer, He has thus fulfilled. Repent therefore, and be converted that your sins may be blotted out, so that times of refreshing may come from the presence of the Lord, and that He may send Jesus Christ, who was preached to you before whom heaven must receive until the times of restoration of all things, which God has spoken by the mouth of all His holy prophets since the world began. [v.24] Yes, and all the prophets from Samuel and those who follow, as many as have spoken, have also foretold these days."

When Peter mentioned Samuel it really peaked my interest. I wanted to know what Samuel had to say about Jesus so I went back and reread first and second Samuel. I read through the first book of Samuel and there was nothing said about Him, and there was nothing in the second book of Samuel until I got to the deliverance chapter toward the end of the book. Many would probably miss the prophetic significance of this chapter but, the true believer could grasp it. Why? Because Jesus said to His disciples, "...

it has been given to you to know the mysteries of the kingdom of heaven…"Matthew 13.11.

The prophet David is speaking in 2Samuel chapter 22, and identifies who he is talking about in verses 2-4. He said, "The Lord is my Rock and my fortress and my Deliverer. The God of my strength in whom I will trust; my shield and the horn of my salvation, my stronghold and my refuge; my Savior, You save me from violence. I will call upon the Lord, who is worthy to be praised; so shall I be saved from my enemies."

We would recognize that our Rock and our Savior is Jesus. Those words, "…You save me from violence" is something our generation can identify with. Jesus said, "as it was in the days of Noah so also will the coming of the Son of Man be." In Genesis 6.11 it said this about Noah's time. "The earth also was corrupt before God and the earth was filled with violence."

Going back to 2Samuel 22.17 it speaks prophetically about the mystery of deliverance. "He sent from above, He took me, He drew me out of many waters. [v.18] He delivered me…" Does the rapture need to be portrayed with an analogy any better than this? I don't think so. Being drawn "out of many waters" is symbolism for being taken out from many peoples. Now in verse 20 notice where to. "He brought me out into a broad place; He delivered me because He delighted in me." So why be taken to a broad place? In the Hebrew it also tends to mean a good place.

Well notice what it says about those who are raptured in Revelation 5.9. "...You are worthy to take the scroll and open its seals; for You were slain and have redeemed us to God by Your blood out of every tribe and tongue and people and nation." Then in verse 11 it says, "Then I looked and I heard the voice of many angels around the throne, the living creatures, and the elders; and the number of them was ten thousand times ten thousand and thousands of thousands." So you see a broad expansive place is needed to accommodate so many in one place.

Notice what Jesus says, in Revelation 22.17, at the time of His coming. "And behold I am coming quickly and <u>My reward is with Me to give</u> to everyone according to his work." Now notice what it says in verse 21 in 2Samuel 22. "<u>The Lord rewarded me</u> according to my righteousness; according to the cleanness of my hands He has recompensed me."

So Peter was correct when he deduced that in the book of Samuel it spoke of Jesus, and in Acts 3.21 that Jesus would bring about the restoration of all things. What has to be restored is bringing us back from a fallen state to a state of perfection once again. In John 17.23 Jesus prayed for this to happen. And John said, "...we know that when He is revealed we shall be like Him, for we shall see Him as He is" 1John3.2.

So Peter wanted his audience to know that Jesus wasn't someone you could dismiss as being out of sight - out of mind. His healing of the lame man was evidence Jesus was very much alive.

Chapter Sixteen
The Ten Horns of The Fourth Beast

Until recently, prophecy scholars have missed an important part of the prophetic picture. First let me state what prophecy students have got right. The fourth beast of Daniel 7.7, 23 represented the region of the old Roman empire. In the end-time ten horns were to emerge from this same region. But the next part, prophecy students got wrong in believing that ten of the horns represented ten nations from that region of the old Roman empire. Daniel 7.24 tells us we should be looking for 10 kings that shall arise not 10 nations. The verse reads, "The ten horns are ten kings who shall arise from this kingdom..."

Some might argue that some of those European nations already have kings which is true and I would add that since they are already kings over their respective countries they then already have their own kingdoms. So why is this a problem? Revelation 17.12 says the following: "The ten horns which you saw are ten kings who have received no kingdom as yet but they receive authority for one hour as kings with the beast.

So what we should expect to see are ten men who have great power probably in the form of great wealth that are pushing for a one world government, and that will arise from the region of the old Roman empire. In the book of James chapter 5 verses 1-8 it indicates they are rich and in verse three it says, "You have heaped up treasure in the last days." The time component here places them in our generation - "last days." The word heaped, in the Greek, means amassed. The first part of verse three indicates the type of wealth they amassed is gold and silver. Every once in a while you will hear of a depository with a basement containing literally tons of gold bars. Do you think there is a connection here?

The scripture says they acquired their wealth through fraudulent means (v.4) even to the point of having people killed (v.6). James describes them as having hearts and minds which are evil as does the Septuagint Bible in Daniel 7.24. There it reads, "As for its ten horns ten kings shall arise and another shall arise behind them who shall surpass in evil all the previous ones." Yes, they are evil and the antichrist will be even more evil than they.

So when is all this supposed to be fulfilled? Well, again in James 5.3 it said in the "last days" and in verse 8 when "the coming of the Lord is at hand." In other words, the generation we are living in. Daniel 7.24 also says, "The ten are ten horns who shall <u>arise</u> from this kingdom. That word "arise" means to appoint; to set up; make to stand. So who does the selecting and appointing of these ten? Will it be through the Bilderburgers, the European Union, the UN? The point is, there will be 10 who will rule over ten regions in the progression toward world government. This step is accomplished **before** the antichrist emerges to his prominent position.

Secondly, you need to see even though they have great power, authority has to be given to them before they can rule (Rev.17.12). Who gives them this authority? It is interesting that after they have been given this authority they in-turn give their full support to the beast or the antichrist. Revelation 17.13 says, "These are of one mind and they will give their power and authority to the beast." Did you notice, from this verse, that they weren't given power. They already had that. All they needed was authority to act.

From Revelation chapter 17 we know they will already be established with power and authority to help bring about the final collapse of the United States so they can rule over 10 regions of the earth. I covered this in my first book (Daniel's Commentary on Bible Prophecy) in chapter 17. So we need to keep watch of anything that will bring about the establishment of these ten. I repeat that these ten are established before the antichrist is revealed.

What will cause the emergence of these ten? I think it will be distress of nations that Jesus spoke of and that is usually the result of failing economies, inflated currencies and the pressure of expanding conflicts and now the large movement of immigrants.

Chapter Seventeen
Unfolding Mystery at Jacob's Trouble

We can view the timing of Jacob's trouble from Jeremiah 30.3-7. It reads, "For behold the days are coming, says the Lord, that I will bring back My people Israel <u>and</u> Judah, says the Lord. And I will cause them to return to the land that I gave their fathers and they shall possess it." Since this was fulfilled in the 1948 generation we know we are talking about the last days here.

From verse five we advance in time to the great tribulation period. Verses 5-7 read, "For thus says the Lord: 'We have heard a voice of trembling, of fear and not of peace. Ask now and see, whether a man is ever in labor with child? So why do I see every man with his hands on his loins like a woman in labor, and all faces turned pale? Alas! For that day is great so that none is like it; and **it is the time of Jacob's trouble**, <u>but he shall be saved out of it</u>.'"

Did you notice from verse six, only males are being addressed here, and secondly, they are promised not to have to go through the time of Jacob's trouble as they would be saved out of it.

This time is addressed again in Isaiah 66.7-8. It says, "Before she was in labor, she gave birth; before her pain came <u>she delivered a male child</u>. Who has heard such a thing? Who has seen such things? Shall the earth be made to give birth in one day? Or shall a nation be born at once? For as soon as Zion was in labor she gave birth to her children." The word "children" here actually reads as "sons" in the NASV Bible - yes, as males. So we see here the male child, in the singular, is being represented in the plural as sons.

When you get to Revelation chapter 12 you see a similar scene with the woman and the man child. The setting here is also at the time of Jacob's trouble. Most get the symbolism of verse one correct when they say the woman with the twelve stars represents Israel. But when they get to the male child of verse five they get it wrong by saying that this represents Jesus. Verse five says, "She bore a male child who was to rule all nations with a rod of iron. And her child was caught up to God and His throne."

First of all, for the child to be Jesus the woman in verse one would have to be represented as Mary, not Israel, but she isn't. Mary has never been portrayed in scripture as being clothed with the sun, the moon under her feet and with a crown of twelve stars.

The next problem we have with the child being Jesus comes from verse four where the dragon stood ready to devour the child as soon as it was born. Yes, there was a threat on Jesus' life by king Herod but it wasn't as soon as Jesus was born but roughly two years later when the wise men arrived from the east to see Him.

The third problem with this child being Jesus is that verse five says her child was caught up to

God and His throne. Jesus was taken up into heaven after He finished His ministry, but He most certainly wasn't a child when it happened. Neither was Jesus taken up into heaven in the middle of the tribulation as this child is. We know this because the woman who gives birth to the child flees into the wilderness (v.6) for one thousand two hundred and sixty days" which remain of the tribulation time.

So to be consistent with the way this passage is being interpreted, if the woman, in the singular, represents a plurality of individuals then the man child, in the singular can also represent a plurality of individuals. The old testament scriptures we looked at previously supports that this is the case. The woman represents the non-Messianic religious Jews who flee into the wilderness. I believe the man child represents the 144,000 and here's why.

In Revelation chapter eleven we found the two witnesses in Israel witnessing. So the expected results of their witnessing would be converts, yes new believers, babes in Christ. And when did the two witnesses finish their ministry? It was finished at the midpoint of the tribulation period just prior to the man child being caught up to heaven. Who were their converts, these new believers in Christ? They are the 144,000 represented as the man child, and who are delivered out of Jacob's trouble.

In Daniel 12.1 it mentions that those who are delivered out of the time of Jacob's trouble are those whose names are "found written in the book." We know people's names are written in the Book of Life when they accept Christ as Savior, so if these 144,000 had their names written in the Book of Life prior to the beginning of the tribulation time they would have been part of the Church. Jesus doesn't leave part of the Church behind at the rapture to do more unfinished witnessing. So this shows they were instead converts in the tribulation time.

Revelation chapter 14 (verses 4-5) show they are caught up to God and to His throne just like it said in Revelation chapter 12 and verse 5, and they are also declared to be males as the scriptures in the old testament said they would be.

The timing fits as well. In chapter 14 they are in heaven just before the proclamation of the angel (vv.9-10) that those on earth are not to take the mark of the beast (and it is not required until the last 3 ½ years of the tribulation).

Return to the woman in Revelation chapter 12 and notice something very interesting about her flight into the wilderness. In verse five it says, "Then the woman fled into the wilderness where she had a place prepared by God…" Then in verse 14 it says, "But the woman was given two wings of a great eagle, that she might fly into the wilderness to her place.

The idea that she is given wings that she might fly would imply there are numerous jumbo jets waiting to take these Jews into the wilderness to safety. Since the antichrist is already in Israel with his army it isn't very likely he would give the airport a pass. On the contrary, he isn't allowing her to escape but rather is trying to prevent it (v.15). So what we find is a hidden meaning in the statement that she is given two wings. We need to unpack the symbolism.

We find a parallel statement given by God after Israel had come out of Egypt in Exodus 19.4. It reads, "You have seen what I did to the Egyptians, and how I bore you on eagles wings and brought you to Myself." They didn't have airplanes back then so we know they didn't fly but something supernatural did happen and we understand what that was, from Isaiah 40.28-29, 31. It reads, "Have you not known? Have you not heard? The everlasting God, the Lord, the Creator of the ends of the earth, neither faints nor is weary. His understanding is unsearchable. He gives power to the weak and to those who have no might He increases strength. But those who wait upon the Lord shall renew their strength; they shall mount up with wings like eagles. They shall run and not be weary, they shall walk and not faint."

How was their departure from Egypt described? Exodus 14.5 says, "Now it was told the king of Egypt that the people had fled..." Another clue revealing the speed at which they traveled was, they weren't even to think about baking any bread with leaven in it for seven days. When you consider the distance they had to travel before crossing the Red Sea it would have required them to travel a minimum of 38 to 40 miles a day - an impossible feat for seven days if you didn't leave anyone behind. But God gave them supernatural strength for seven days to do just that. Pharaoh's army had to use horses and chariots just to catch up.

So when you see the phrase in Revelation 12.14 that the woman will be given wings as an eagle you know that it likely means, one more time, God is going to supply the woman with supernatural strength to make her escape into the wilderness.

But here is where we run into another interesting parallel. Verse 15 says, "And the serpent poured water like a river out of his mouth after the woman so that he might cause her to be swept away with the flood." So what is this symbolic flood that is pursuing the woman? It is the antichrist's forces and the earth opens up supernaturally and swallows them. The same was true of Pharaoh's army in that in pursuing Israel they were also swallowed up in the sea and destroyed.

It is also interesting to note that when the children of Israel got to the wilderness God fed them supernaturally with manna and the woman mentioned in Revelation 12 is to be fed by God as well.

Chapter Eighteen
The Last Trumpet

In the past there has been some controversy over hen the sounding of the last trumpet takes place. he sounding of the last trumpet being supposedly in reference to when the saints are caught up. One person has said, "Well it's a no brainer. During the time of the seven trumpet judgments when the seventh one sounds that is the last one." Actually it isn't the last one as we will see in a moment.

First of all, we should not confuse the time of judgments and the time of deliverance. The seventh trumpet deals with judgment not with deliverance of the saints.

We need to look at the statement the apostle Paul made in 1Corinthians 15.51-52. "Behold I tell you a mystery: We shall not all sleep, but we shall all be changed - in a moment, in the twinkling of an eye, at the last trumpet. For the trumpet will sound and the dead will be raised incorruptible, and we shall be changed."

I probably should have quoted verse 50 as well as it establishes who Paul is talking about and that is all those who will inherit the kingdom of God right down to the last of them. Maybe we can understand this a little bit better by asking a question. Will Daniel's people, the Jews, who have their names written in the Book of Life inherit the kingdom of God? The answer is yes. Will the Bride of Christ, the Church, inherit the kingdom of God? Again, the answer is yes. Will the great tribulation saints inherit the kingdom of God? The answer is yes as they are the final ingathering of the Feast of Harvest, the good harvest, and these in particular, are the ones who hear the "last trumpet call."

Jesus pointed out that this is when the last call is sounded in Matthew 24.29-31 and it is understood by the context that it isn't happening in the middle of the tribulation but at the end of it.

Let's read those three verses. "Immediately after the tribulation of those days the sun will be darkened, and the moon will not give its light; the stars will fall from heaven, and the powers of the heavens will be shaken. Then the sign of the Son of Man will appear in heaven, and then all the tribes of the earth will mourn and they will see the Son of Man coming on the clouds of heaven with power and great glory. And He will send His angels **with a great sound of a trumpet**, and they will gather together His elect from the four winds, from one end of heaven to the other."

There is something else to be picked up on from the Corinthian chapter 15 passage. Did you notice the main theme Paul was focusing on was that of being "changed" from mortality to immortality at the last trump. So what Paul was saying there was that those (the last to inherit the kingdom) will be the last ones to be changed and receive immortality. Paul really isn't addressing a pretrib rapture in this passage but of those who will be changed.

In a different letter Paul does address a pretrib rapture in 1Thessalonians 4.16-17. "For the Lord Himself will descend from heaven with a shout, with the voice of an archangel, and with **the trumpet** of God, and the dead in Christ will rise first. Then we who are alive and remain shall be caught up together with them in the clouds to meet the Lord in the air. And thus we shall always be with the Lord."

You observed the word "trumpet" used here with the catching away of the saints but what was missing? It was the word "last" because this pretrib rapture trumpet call is not the last one. The last one comes at the end of the tribulation not prior to it.

Chapter Nineteen
Wonders That Shoot Forth

For years I wondered about the meaning of the scripture found in Joel 2.30 but now I believe it has given up its secret. It reads, "And I will show wonders in the heavens and in the earth; blood and fire and pillars of smoke."

The word "show" in the Hebrew is "nathan" and can have a wide variety of meanings. This word can mean "cause," "grant," "lift up," "shoot forth," "strike," and "bring forth."

This brings us to the next word which is "wonders." It also can have other meanings and the one most often read is "signs." The Septuagint Bible probably renders it best when it uses the word "portent." In other words, what will be seen and experienced may be bad but after this even worse things will happen.

Now when I first read Joel 2.30 I thought well this must be speaking about volcanic eruptions where you have belching lava and pillars of smoke and I suppose one could still hold to that view but I'm inclined now to believe it is speaking about something else. You see there are volcanoes erupting around the world all the time but they really don't account for the word "blood" because most of the time people have enough prior warning to get away from an eruption.

In the context of this verse, the word "blood" is significant because it represents loss of life. Knowing this we then realize this is talking about much more than viewing a lunar eclipse because that doesn't cause loss of life. But there is something that fits this criteria and it is exploding nuclear warheads from missiles.

If we use acceptable alternate Hebrew meanings in verse 30 it might read; And I will grant (or allow) portents in the heavens and in the earth; blood and fire and pillars of smoke.

This is definitely an event that would cause a large loss of life. The fireball from a nuclear explosion would incinerate every thing in a one mile radius and start fires out to a 15 mile radius from just a small four megaton bomb. Immediately afterward you have a towering pillar of smoke that forms a mushroom cloud.

If you noticed, from this verse, it is not depicting a solitary event because the word "pillars" is in the plural. This indicates many such events are happening at this time. Also according to the sequence of events in Joel chapter two it shows this will occur before the "awesome day of the Lord" which will be even worse than the foregoing nuclear exchange.

The Lord is giving us important information as to how awful or terrible the day of the Lord will be. We know these words in Joel were written for our generation because only our generation has knowledge of what devastation can be brought about by a nuclear missile so we know we are living in the generation in which this will occur.

Verse 31 tells us what happens after these missiles come down out of the heavens or the sky to do their destructive work. The verse reads, "The sun shall be turned into darkness and the moon into blood..." Scientists have said that a large nuclear exchange could cause a nuclear winter from the radiated debris that would go up into the atmosphere and the darkened skies would make the moon look blood red.

There are a growing number of nations with this nuclear capability such as: Red China, Russia, North Korea, Pakistan, the UK, the U.S., India, France and Israel. Iran is also striving to be in this elite group. These nations circle the earth with their nuclear capability and if they all got involved in a WWIII conflict this would produce a global phenomenon unlike anything this world has ever seen before. Is it likely? Unfortunately the answer is yes. Why? Because if one of those nuclear powers was left unharmed they would then become the dominate world power and the other nuclear powers would not allow this. This is what I was told when going through my nuclear power training for the Navy.

It is just amazing that the Bible continues to inform us of future events, that will take place in our generation well before they happen. Can't say we haven't been informed.

Chapter Twenty
Ancient Prophecies About Christ

We will see why it is significant to look at some of the foretold prophecies about Christ.

There was a prophecy recorded by Moses, but given by the prophet Balaam about 1400 B.C. declaring where the promised One would appear. In the book of Numbers chapter 24 verse 17 it says, "I see Him, but not now; I behold Him, but not near; a Star shall come out of Jacob; a Scepter shall rise out of Israel..." This prophecy points both to His first coming and to His second coming in which He will be given the scepter to rule and reign.

We see the fulfillment of the first part of this prophecy in the book of Matthew chapter two verses one and two. It reads, "Now after Jesus was born in Bethlehem of Judea in the days of Herod the king, behold wise men from the East came to Jerusalem, saying, 'Where is He who has been born King of the Jews? For we have seen **His star** in the East and have come to worship Him.'"

Yes, Jesus rose out of the land of Israel just as prophesied - not out of another land which would have nullified the prophecy.

In the book of Deuteronomy chapter 18 and verse 15 Moses prophesies of the promised One to come. Moses says, "The Lord your God will raise up for you a Prophet like me from your midst, from your brethren, Him you shall hear." This prophecy declared that the promised One to come would also be a prophet and be of the Jewish people. So was Jesus a Jew? Yes, He was from the tribe of Judah. We also know that Jesus gave many prophecies that are even yet today still being fulfilled, but two in particular show Him to be a true prophet.

The first is, He prophesied that if the temple of His body was destroyed He would raise it up in three days (John 2.19). This was fulfilled when He rose from the dead three days after He was crucified and His resurrection was even attested to by angels. Luke 24.1-7 gives the account but reading from verse six the angel says, "He is not here, but is risen! Remember how He spoke to you when He was still in Galilee, saying 'The Son of Man must be delivered into the hands of sinful men, and be crucified and the third day rise again.'"

The next prophecy we find being given by Jesus in Matthew 24.1-2. It reads, "Then Jesus went out and departed from the temple, and His disciples came up to show Him the buildings of the temple. And Jesus said to them, Do you not see all these things? Assuredly, I say to you, not one stone shall be left here upon another, that shall not be thrown down." This was fulfilled in 70 A.D. by the Roman soldiers. Both prophecies were fulfilled precisely as Jesus said! How precise? Well there wasn't even one stone left on another as Jesus said. Yes, Jesus fulfilled Moses' prophecy that the Messiah would be a prophet who spoke the words of God (Deut.18.17-18).

Now these prophecies that we have looked at so far have been given for the purpose of identifying who the promised One would be when He came. This is very important because it was linked to why He was to come. When Adam and Eve sinned they could do nothing but perpetuate the human race in a fallen sinful state. God cared about that and said that He would send One to redeem mankind from their fallen state. That is why there are so many prophecies concerning this One that was to come so He would be recognized when He came.

There is another prophecy, given by Job, which showed he felt he needed a Redeemer. Job said, "For I know that my Redeemer lives, and He shall stand at last on the earth; and after my skin is destroyed this I know, that in my flesh I shall see God" (Job 19.25-26). Job recognized that his Redeemer would be Deity. There is no way man could redeem a fallen race - only God could do it.

The sacrifice our Redeemer would make was prophetically given over 780 years before it happened. A very detailed account is given by the prophet Isaiah in chapter 53, but I will summarize some of the specifics. From verse four we read, "Surely He has borne our griefs and carried our sorrows; yet we esteemed Him stricken, smitten by God, and afflicted. But He was wounded for our transgressions, He was bruised for our iniquities; the chastisement for our peace was upon Him, and by His stripes we are healed. [v.6] All we like sheep have gone astray; we have turned everyone to his own way; and the Lord has laid on Him the iniquity of us all. [v.7] He was oppressed and He was afflicted, yet He opened not His mouth; He was led as a lamb to the slaughter... [v.8] ...For He was cut off from the land of the living... [v.10]...You made His soul an offering for sin..."

Yes, this was fulfilled about 780 years later when Jesus was crucified on the cross. The account depicting the fulfillment of Isaiah's prophecy can be read in the book of Matthew chapter 27 verses 27-51, and it was **all** fulfilled exactly as prophesied. **What do you do with 100% accuracy?** No other person has had such profound prophecies given about them as those given about Jesus! No one!

There is another prophecy that addresses Christ haters and they should be aware of it. It is given by the prophet David in Psalm 2.7-12. It reads, "I will declare the decree: The Lord (Jehovah) has said to Me, You are My Son, today I have begotten You. Ask of Me, and I will give You the nations for Your inheritance, and the ends of the earth for Your possession. You shall break them with a rod of iron; You shall dash them to pieces like a potter's vessel. Now therefore be wise O kings; be instructed, you judges of the earth, serve the Lord with fear, and rejoice with trembling. Kiss the Son lest He be angry, and you perish in the way, when His wrath is kindled but a little. Blessed are those who put their trust in Him."

The Muslims would say, Allah doesn't have a son and they are absolutely right - he doesn't, but Jehovah does. Therefore, Allah and Jehovah are not the same God. If you noticed in verse two it is Jehovah that is speaking and He declares He has a Son. So the question is how long will God's declarations be tested before they are believed?

Chapter Twenty One
America - Be Aware

This chapter is intended to provide some initial identification for America in scripture from Isaiah 47 and Revelation 17. We will look at two references; the first from Revelation.

Revelation 17.3, 5 "So he carried me away in the Spirit into the wilderness. And I saw a woman sitting on a scarlet beast which was full of names of blasphemy, having seven heads and ten horns. And on her forehead a name was written: MYSTERY BABYLON THE GREAT, THE MOTHER OF HARLOTS AND OF THE ABOMINATIONS OF THE EARTH."

Isaiah 47.1 "Come down and sit in the dust O virgin daughter of Babylon; sit on the ground without a throne O daughter of the Chaldeans! For you shall no more be called tender and delicate."

The word "Babylon" is being used to identify the woman in both the old and new testament passages. This is another clue that the scripture isn't referring to historical Babylon of Nebuchadnezzar or Belshazzar's day. You see the lion was always symbolical of historical Babylon not a woman. But the statue of Liberty is the symbol of a woman the world over associates with America.

The use of the word "Babylon" though does infer a nation is being alluded to. In both passages of

Revelation and Isaiah we are viewing the moral and spiritual condition as it is, in its declining stages in the end time. The word "Babylon" itself means confusion. In today's society what is causing confusion? Could it be redefining what constitutes a marriage? Could it be what is known as political correctness where voicing what God says are abominations to Him are now considered hate speech? Is it putting a verbal spin on what is evil and wrong and calling it ok? Is it suppressing scientific discoveries that reveal the Bible is true after all? Is it bribing the justice system to cover up crimes of hate and greed? Is it slaughtering the unborn because they are not deemed to be human? Do I need to make this list any longer to make my point?

I found it interesting that the word "confusion" also means "wilderness." In both cases, the woman in Isaiah and Revelation are experiencing wilderness conditions. The word "wilderness" means uncultured and uncultivated. What does uncultured imply? It implies those who are not tolerant, not given to respect, not well educated. Does this remind you of those who graduate from high school that still can't read? What about those given to rioting and violent protests? What about those who prey on the weak such as those who play the knockout game? What happened to respect and politeness? I believe we have a great deal of evidence that our society is becoming very uncultured.

Another thing that needs to be seen from the Revelation passage is that while the nation has declined to a wilderness condition the governing authorities have essentially fleeced the populace. The government has provided well for itself. Notice Revelation 17.4 says, "The woman was arrayed in purple and scarlet, and adorned with gold and precious stones and pearls having in her hand a golden cup full of abominations and the filthiness of her fornication." I just don't see where the government has sacrificed for the people here?

I do see where the government turns on its own people. In verse six it reads, "I saw the woman drunk with the blood of the saints and with the blood of the martyrs of Jesus..." In the year 2015 the Department of Homeland Security coordinated with the military (special ops) in training exercises (called Jade Helm 15) for the purpose of rounding up civilians who they will deem to be a threat to society and the government.

Are we not seeing Bible prophecy being fulfilled right before our eyes? The government has not figured the rapture of the Bride of Christ into their plans though.

The saints being killed (in Rev. 17.6) are great tribulation saints - not the Bride of Christ. So it is important for people to realize they need to be serious about their relationship with Christ or they won't be going in the rapture. It is about to make a real difference for those who have set their affection of things above and not on the things of earth! Narrow is the way that leads to life. Few that find it!

Chapter Twenty Two
The Mystery of The Stars Falling

When reading about the opening of the seals in Revelation chapter six it has been assumed that the next seal wouldn't be opened until the first seal had been fulfilled.

It turns out this isn't isn't the way it works. The first seal should have tipped us off.

For example, the first seal reveals the antichrist to the world, but the antichrist's exploits continue on for seven years. Now all the seal judgments, trumpet judgments, and bowl judgments must be fulfilled in that same seven year period of time. We see therefore, that the seals will all be opened relatively soon to each other but their events are phased in over a period of time. In fact some of the events under the sixth seal aren't fully realized until toward the end of the tribulation period. Knowing this is key!

Now let's go to Matthew 24 where Jesus is providing His disciples a lot of information on the end time and in verse 21 He says that there will be severe tribulation. When you get to verse 29 He says, "Immediately after the tribulation of those days the sun will be darkened, and the moon will not give its light; the stars will fall from heaven, and the powers of the heavens will be shaken." So Jesus is telling what happens toward the end of the tribulation. Then in Revelation 6.12-13 Jesus again tells the apostle

John what will happen. John said, "I looked when He opened the sixth seal, and behold there was a great earthquake; and the sun became black as sackcloth of hair, and the moon became like blood. And the stars of heaven fell to the earth, as a fig tree drops its late figs when it is shaken by a mighty wind."

When it says the "stars of heaven fell to the earth" I believe is a poor translation. A better translation would say, that the stars of heaven fell <u>toward</u> the earth. This is acceptable in the Greek although it would not be a common rendering and is probably why it wasn't used.

Now if you want to shake up people who observe the stars in the sky just start moving stars around and see how excited they will get. Well that is what is happening here and it marks a colossal change from the norm. Many of these stars will appear to move directly toward the earth (reversing their expansion mode they are in presently).

After the time of God's indignation (i.e. His wrath), this is again described in Isaiah 34.2-4 but we only need to quote verse four. It says, "All the host of heaven shall be dissolved and the heavens shall be rolled up like a scroll; all their host shall fall down as the leaf falls from the vine, and as fruit falling from a fig tree." The word "dissolved" here means to melt away and then it vanishes.

Even though the inhabitants of the earth will see the beginning of these celestial events happening at the end of the great tribulation time they won't be completed until after the reign of Christ (2Peter 3.10-13).

When you get to Revelation chapter 12 it also speaks of falling stars but this is completely different in its representation, and in the time period involved. In verse three it is speaking of Satan as the dragon and in verse four it says, "his tail drew a third of the stars of heaven and threw them to the earth..." We get an explanation when we read verses 7-9. "And war broke out in heaven: Michael and his angels fought, but they did not prevail nor was a place found for them in heaven any longer. So the great dragon was cast out, that serpent of old, called the Devil and Satan, who deceives the whole world; he was cast to the earth, and his angels were cast out with him."

Yes, these represented as stars fallen to the earth are the Devil's angels. We know the time frame when this happens is at the closing out of the first half of the tribulation. We know this because what follows are religious Jews bolting for the wilderness where they will be for 1260 days (in v.6) which is for the last 3 ½ years of the great tribulation.

This symbolism of angels being represented as stars has precedent. In Revelation 9.1 it says, "...And I saw a star fallen to the earth. To him was given the key to the bottomless pit." Also in Daniel 12.3 it says, "Those who are wise shall shine like the brightness of the firmament and those who turn many to righteousness like the stars forever and ever.

If we bring in the two witnesses from chapter 11 into this picture we will discover something quite interesting. If you review Daniel 12.11 you will see the two witnesses begin their ministry in Israel (Malachi 4.5) 30 days before the antichrist is revealed or 30 days before the opening of the first seal. We also know from Revelation 11.3 that their ministry is only for 1260 days or 3 ½ years before they are translated back to heaven. So what happens immediately after they are translated? The answer is in verses 14-15. It says, "The second woe is past; behold the third woe is coming quickly. Then the <u>seventh</u> angel sounded…" This tells us the two witnesses were on earth through the first six trumpet judgments which were <u>initiated in the first 3 ½</u> years of the seven year period.

So again, the seal judgments and the first six trumpet judgments fall under the first 3 ½ years of the tribulation time. This helps put the timing of these judgment events into better focus.

Chapter Twenty Three
War of Ezekiel 38 & 39 Versus Armageddon

Preparation for the battle of Armageddon occurs under the sixth bowl judgment (Rev.16.12-14, 16). "Then the sixth angel poured out his bowl on the great river Euphrates, and its water was dried up, so that the way of the kings from the east might be prepared. And I saw three unclean spirits like frogs coming out of the mouth of the dragon, out of the mouth of the beast, and out of the mouth of the false prophet. For they are spirits of demons, performing signs, which go out to the kings of the earth, and of the whole world, to gather them to the battle of that great day of God Almighty. [v.16] And they gathered them together to the place called in Hebrew, Armageddon."

I am convinced, from scripture, that the war mentioned in Ezekiel 38 and 39, and the war of Armageddon are the same war. Why? They are both described as being the final conflict before Jesus reigns as King on earth. So if they weren't the same war then one of them couldn't be the final conflict, and that would pose a problem in the timing. The accounts have eerie similarities but also each account provides unique information just as the accounts in Matthew, Mark, Luke, and John did relative to each other.

For example, in Ezekiel 38 are listed specific nations involved in the battle against Israel but it doesn't list them all. Verse nine says, "You will ascend, coming like a storm, covering the land like a cloud, you and all your troops and many peoples with you." In the Ezekiel account it listed those nations by name that are coming to wipe out Israel. But there are other nations that are going to be involved in this battle but for a different reason.

You see, it is from Daniel chapter eleven and verse 44 that we find the antichrist has enemies outside of Israel and they are coming to eliminate the antichrist. That is why the antichrist positions himself in Israel hoping the remaining Jews will be killed in this great conflict at that time.

Daniel 11.44-45, a passage that alludes to this reads, "But news from the east and the north shall trouble him; therefore he shall go out with great fury to destroy and annihilate many. And he shall plant the tents of his palace between the seas and the glorious holy mountain; yet he shall come to his end, and no one will help him."

Now let's look at similarities for the Ezekiel war and Armageddon. Both accounts mention a very great earthquake. Ezekiel 38.19-20 reads, "For in My jealousy and in the fire of My wrath I have spoken" Surely in that day there shall be a great earthquake in the land of Israel, so that the fish of the sea, the birds of the heavens, the beasts of the field, all creeping things that creep upon the earth, and all men who are on the face of the earth shall shake at My presence. The mountains shall be thrown down, the steep places shall fall, and every wall shall fall to the ground."

Now under the seventh bowl judgment when the war of Armageddon rages, Revelation 16.18, 20 reads, "And there were noises and thunderings and lightnings; and there was a great earthquake, such a mighty and great earthquake, as had not occurred since men were on the earth. Then every island fled away and the mountains were not found."

Besides the similarity of the two earthquake accounts there is the problem with the mountains being thrown down. If the mountains are thrown down in the Ezekiel account then there shouldn't still be mountains to be thrown down at the time of the battle of Armageddon. Therefore the timing of these battles are the same.

The next similarity are great hailstones. Ezekiel 38.22 reads, "And I will bring him to judgment with pestilence and blood shed; I will rain down on him, on his troops, and on the many peoples who are with him flooding rain, <u>great hailstones</u>, fire and brimstone."

In Revelation 16.21 (still under the 7th bowl judgment) it reads, "And great hail from heaven fell upon men, each hailstone about the weight of a talent. Men blasphemed God because of the plague of the hail, since that plague was exceedingly great."

The next similarity is God's sacrificial meal for the birds and the beasts. Ezekiel 39.17-18, 20 reads, "And as for you Son of Man, thus says the Lord God, speak to every sort of bird and to every beast of the field; assemble yourselves and come; gather together from all sides to My sacrificial meal which I am sacrificing for you, a great sacrificial meal on the mountains of Israel, the you may eat flesh and drink blood. You shall eat the flesh of the mighty, drink the blood of the princes of the earth...[v.20] You shall be filled at My table with horses, and riders, with mighty men and with all the men of war, says the Lord God."

In Revelation 19.17-18 it says, "Then I saw an angel standing in the sun; and he cried with a loud voice, saying to all the birds that fly in the midst of heaven, 'come and gather together for the supper of the great God, that you may eat the flesh of kings, the flesh of captains, the flesh of mighty men the flesh of horses and of those who sit on them, and the flesh of all people, free and slave, both small and great."

After God retaliates against the armies fighting against Israel He makes a statement (Ezekiel 39.7) and says, "So I will make My holy name known in the midst of my people Israel and I will not let them profane My holy name anymore. Then the nations shall know that I am the LORD, the Holy One in Israel." This statement convinces me that the war described here in Ezekiel 38 & 39 is the last war, that of Armageddon, from that phrase "I will not let them profane My holy name anymore."

To understand what I am getting at we need to understand the word "profane." So how would one profane the name of the Lord? And what does that mean? First of all, it would be some kind of outward manifestation and in this case it would most likely be verbal and could be followed by a gesture such as a frown, a shaking of the head or just walking away from discussing the Lord. Have you ever noticed that when a Jew is discussing religion in any way that he avoids the name of Jesus crossing his lips? He may say Messiah or Yeshua but almost never the name of Jesus. You see if they should say the name of Jesus, by its own meaning of the name, it means Savior, and they cannot acknowledge that Jesus is Savior.

So according to the last phrase I quoted <u>not</u> profaning the name of the Lord would mean the nations <u>would then know</u> that Jesus is acknowledged as Lord by the very nation that should be acknowledging it. That was one purpose for the nation of Israel (Exodus 19.5-6; Isaiah 49.6).

Now let's go to the time of the triumphal entry (Luke 19.28-44). The disciples following Jesus were voicing praise to Jesus when some of the Pharisees cried out to Jesus to rebuke them. Why? Because they considered it blasphemy that He should receive praise only meant for God. Then in verse 41 it says, "Now as He drew near, He saw the city and wept over it." And in verse 44 the reason is given; "...because you did not know the time of your visitation." This was prophesied by Isaiah in chapter 53 verse 3. It says, "He is despised and rejected by men, a Man of sorrows and acquainted with grief and we hid as it were our faces from Him; He was despised, and we did not esteem Him." So what part of the definition of "profane" was this? We recognize it as sorrow. And was it verbal? Yes. Was He heartbroken (another definition of sorrow)? Yes. Did His heart feel wounded? Yes. And on the cross His heart was even pierced (one definition of profane meaning to "bore" into).

Now let's go to one of the first definitions of the word profane which is to break as to break one's word. Well what was the covenant word that Israel was to keep? When asked what the greatest commandment was, Jesus replied (in Matthew 22.37) "You shall love the Lord your God with all your heart, with all your soul, and with all your mind." So Israel broke this commandment when they had Jesus crucified. You don't crucify someone if you love them only if you hate them. So by not loving Jesus as Lord and God Israel has profaned His great name! The last similarity ties into this when Jesus Himself returns where He is visibly seen.

Revelation 19.11-16, 19 reads, "Now I saw heaven opened and behold a white horse. And He who sat on him was called, Faithful and True, and in righteousness He judges and makes war. His eyes were like a flame of fire, and on His head were many crowns. He had a name written that no one knew except Himself. He was clothed with a robe dipped in blood, and His name is called the Word of God. And the armies in heaven, clothed in fine linen, white and clean, followed Him on white horses. Now out of

His mouth goes a sharp sword, that with it He should strike the nations. And He Himself will rule them with a rod of iron. He Himself treads the winepress of the fierceness and wrath of Almighty God. And He has on His robe and on His thigh a name written; KING of KINGS and LORD of LORDS. [v.19] And I saw the beast, the kings of the earth, and their armies gathered together to make war against Him who sat on the horse and against His army."

Then in Ezekiel 38.23 it says, "Thus I will magnify Myself, and I will be known in the eyes of many nations. Then they shall know that I am the Lord." In Ezekiel 39.7 we read earlier the phrase, "the nations shall know that I am the Lord, the Holy One in Israel." Yes, Jesus will be visibly seen at this time, and reveals Himself to the whole word in great glory!

These are the reasons why I conclude that the war mentioned in Ezekiel 38 & 39 will not happen for several years yet and that it is the same war as Armageddon. I expect the Psalm 83 war to be the next big conflict possibly leading to the antichrist confirming the peace covenant with Israel.

Chapter Twenty Four
Age of The Earth - A Falling Away

Does cosmic light determine age of the earth? Scientists say the universe is 13.7 billion years old. The farthest known galaxy MAC0647-JD is 13.3 billion light years away, yet we see it. Therefore it would need to be 13.3 billion years old in which it produced light so that light would have time to reach earth according to the theory. But scientists also say the earth is only 4.54 billion years old.

The conclusion of the scientific data means the light from the furthest galaxies would already be inundating the earth's region with light when the earth came into existence. That means there is no light/age problem with regard to the age of the earth relative to the stars. It means the earth does not have to be old just because stars are far away. The distance the stars are from the earth does not determine the age of the earth.

Defaulting to the Word of God gives us a little different picture of created objects with respect to the earth. When you incorporate the Supra-natural you might expect this. God says that after He created the heavens He stretched them out. Isaiah 42.5 says, "Thus says God the Lord, who created the heavens and stretched them out..." Isaiah 45.12 says, "It is I who made the earth, and created man upon it.

I stretched out the heavens with My hands and I ordained all their host."

So if you have a central location of created luminaries and they are being spread apart from each other to great distances you don't then have to wait billions of years for light to reach you as the light is already at its initial point of origin before it begins moving away from you, and yet, you still see all the lights only they get smaller the farther away they go until, at some point, you then need a telescope to see many of them. God doesn't tell us how fast He moved the luminaries apart only that He did it. So again, there is no light/age distance problem that would require the earth to be billions of years old.

The Gap theory - what does it imply? It implies that when God spoke the earth into existence He left this glob of material in the cosmos for billions of years before deciding to do something with it. It was therefore a veritable wasteland for billions of years. Does the scripture address this? Yes it does in Isaiah 45.18. It says, "For thus says the Lord, who created the heavens (He is the God who formed the earth and made it. He established it, and <u>did not create it a waste place</u>, but formed it to be inhabited), I am the Lord and there is none else." So the verse reveals that at the time He was creating the earth He was visualizing the earth to be a habitable planet. So does it make any sense that God would want to delay His work for a few billion years before completing what He started?

It would seem we have the answer to that in Exodus 20.11. The verse reads, "For in six days the Lord made the heavens and the earth, the sea, and all that is in them, and rested on the seventh day." From this verse it doesn't look like He took any breaks until day seven.

No where in Scripture do we find God taking or requiring eons of time to do creative works. For example, when He made our sun and moon He did it in just one day - on day four - and our sun is so big you could put one million, three hundred thousand earths inside the sun! You are probably aware that scientists say our sun is 4.5-4.6 billion years old. But the Bible tells us it was made within the creation week of seven days. And we know that the beginning of creation week in which Adam was made only goes back a little over 6,000 years. Jesus, Himself, said "But from the beginning of the creation God made them male and female"(Mark 10.6).

So we know from Scripture that Jesus indicated the creation was young. Therefore in dating the sun scientists are off by over 4+ billion years. This reveals scientists have a real problem in establishing ages and frankly I would say they need to find out where they have erred. Why? Well because God was there when everything was created and He gave His account of what He did to Moses who documented it. Our present day scientists were not there!

It begs the question - who's account is most believable? If God can make our sun, a colossus of its size in one day, on day four, He certainly doesn't need eons of time to make the earth. The Scripture reveals there is coming another day when God will create a new heaven and a new earth and it won't take Him long to do it.

Isaiah 65.17-19 reveals God, in the future, will do a new act of creation. It reads, "For behold, I create new heavens and a new earth; and the former shall not be remembered or come to mind. But be glad and rejoice forever in what I create; for behold I create Jerusalem as a rejoicing and her people a joy. I will rejoice in Jerusalem and joy in My people; the voice of weeping shall no longer be heard in her, nor the voice of crying." So did you notice who this new earth and new Jerusalem is created for? Yes, the verse said for God's people.

When will they occupy this new earth? The answer is right after the great white throne judgment mentioned in Revelation 20. What follows next in Revelation 21.1-4 is a confirmation of the prophecy given in Isaiah 65 that we looked at earlier.

Revelation 21.1-4 reads, "Now I saw a new heaven and a new earth, for the first heaven and the first earth had passed away. Also there was no more sea. Then I John saw the holy city New Jerusalem, coming down out of heaven from God prepared as a bride adorned for her husband. And I heard a voice from heaven saying, 'Behold the tabernacle of God is with men, and He will dwell with them, and they shall be His people. God Himself will be with them and be their God. And God will wipe away every tear from their eyes; there shall be no more death, nor sorrow, nor crying, for the former things have passed away.'"

Since Christ's reign on earth will be for 1,000 years and since it commences in our generation it doesn't leave much time in which to create the new earth so eons of time must not be needed.

Chapter Twenty Five
Amazing Encounters

I debated for quite some time what the title of this chapter should be. When God chooses to use people for His purpose He frequently chooses those you would least expect and I believe I fall into that category. What I value the most is my relationship with the Lord and I'm in that minority group of those who choose to believe what God has said in the Bible is true. Evolution just isn't believable!

My first major encounter with the Lord came when I was eight years old. It was in the month of February on a Sunday night at church. At the altar that night I became a born again believer. I literally wept before the Lord for about an hour, and when I arose from the altar I was a changed person. I couldn't get over how light I felt. It was like someone had lifted a heavy load off my shoulders and I felt such love for everyone, and I wanted to tell people about Jesus. Yes, that was an amazing encounter. Little did I know, but there would be another the following night.

The next night while sleeping I had a dream. In the dream I was taken up to heaven and I got to see Jesus. I saw first hand who He was that saved me. As He was walking toward me I couldn't help noticing the Holy City a short distance away and the light of it just glistened with beauty. Heaven was similar to being on earth only everything there was perfect. The colors of everything you looked at were much more vivid than here on earth and there was no pollution of any kind. My time with the Lord was brief but an unforgettable amazing encounter. It was clear, the Lord wanted me to cherish this new relationship with Him.

The next notable encounter came five years later when I was 13 years old. I had a real hunger for the things of God and it was after attending one of A.A. Allen's tent meetings that I heard there was going to be an all night prayer meeting. I had never been to one of those before so I received permission from my parents to go to it. I managed, with a great deal of effort, to stay awake and pray through the night. Little did I know that in the morning a blessing awaited me. I happened to look at my hands and on them was oil. This was no ordinary oil. It glistened and had the most wonderful fragrance; nothing like anything I'd ever experienced before. I began to realize at that point that the Lord's anointing was on my life but it still wasn't apparent to me yet what He had in mind.

At the age of 15 I became hooked on trying to understand Bible prophecy. It was at that point I realized God was using it to confirm His word.

Several more years went by and after completing military service I got married. The church we were attending was wanting more Sunday school teachers so I volunteered to teach an adult class on the book of Revelation. When I started I did not have a developed outline for this class. That meant the lesson I would give the following Sunday was based on the preparation I did for it during the previous week.

There are two instances that stand out during this time of teaching. In my preparation time I came to the fifth trumpet judgment dealing with the locusts that would sting people and the pain would be so bad people would try and commit suicide but death would elude them and they wouldn't die. This mystified me in knowing how to relate this to the class in any meaningful way. So I prayed about it asking the Lord to help the class to understand this. Well the answer came that very week in the news. Someone in California tried to commit suicide by jumping off the Golden Gate bridge and they should have died only they didn't - they still lived.

One of the things that amazed me was when at a later time I taught this Revelation class to a different group of adults when I came to this same place in the study. In that same week of preparation another person jumped off the Golden Gate bridge trying to commit suicide and also lived.

On a more personal level, I had another amazing experience. My morning routine was to arise from bed at 4:00 O'clock in the morning, shower, put on a robe and study for a couple of hours before going off to work. I had been receiving some amazing insight from the Lord in my preparation time and one morning as I was finishing up I heard footsteps of someone in the house and I thought that was odd since my wife was still in bed and I hadn't got up from my chair yet. So I went in to where she was and asked her if she heard anyone walking around and she said she hadn't. So I just forgot about it until the next morning when at the close of my study session I heard footsteps again. This time I was more alert and I noticed the sound of those footsteps came from beside where I was sitting and began going across the room only this time I could actually see the foot impressions being made in the carpet. Then I knew the Lord had been by my side aiding me in my study. Yes, another amazing encounter. It was some time after this that I completed two years at a community college plus two terms at the university that I felt the Lord was nudging me to enroll in Bible college. The Lord had a special way of getting my attention. It went something like this. I would go into the library to do my studying and all of a sudden the Lord would deluge me with a sermon that would be so captivating that I couldn't concentrate on anything else. The Lord knew where my heart was and the secular university wasn't it.

It was now winter and I rented a large U-Haul trailer to pull behind our car. Our destination would change from Springfield Oregon to Springfield Missouri and it would occur in the dead of winter with our two small children. Our route would take us across Wyoming. There had been a lot of snow but the freeway had been cleared for the most part. The timing for our trip was remarkable as if we had started out two days earlier the highway would have been closed to travel. What hadn't been cleared though was access to rest areas and we needed to make a rest area stop. The snow was so deep it was difficult to tell where the road was and we were the only car to pull into it.

When we were ready to leave the rest area the car tires began slipping and the car started to slide off the road a little bit and I knew I would have to put on chains to have any chance of getting out of there. Suddenly two men appeared and asked if they could help us. This surprised me because I didn't know there was anyone else around and we were a long way from any town. In no time at all they had put the chains on the car allowing me to get back on the road. When I turned around to thank them they had disappeared. All I know is that the Lord provided help when I needed it. Yes, another amazing encounter.

It was my senior year in Bible college and aside from my studies Bible prophecy was still my passion. On this particular day I was in the middle of the living room floor with my books spread out around me making it easy to access lexicons, concordances, various Bible translations etc. All of a sudden the room began filling with the presence of the Lord and His Spirit began to permeate every cell in my body and it was the most wonderful feeling I have ever felt. Along with that there was this most fragrant aroma that accompanied His presence and it was the exact same fragrance as when I had the oil on my hands years earlier.

Truly this was the Lord's anointing and I didn't want it to leave but I had no control over it and after a few minutes it lifted. Yes, another amazing encounter, and in none of these encounters was I praying to have any of these experiences. They just happened.

I will tell of one more instance in closing out this chapter. After I left Bible college we moved back to Springfield Oregon where I got a job in a hydraulic manufacturing plant. The Lord placed me here where I could be a witness for Him to people who would never darken the doors of a church. At this plant they made the parts that went into making hydraulic cylinders and my job was in inventory control where I collected the parts from the machines and kept them organized on shelves and then took them to fill orders for the assembly line where cylinders were then assembled.

Inventory control was located upstairs right over the machine shop which made the parts and the machines were very noisy. I recognized that this was an ideal situation in which I could sing praise songs and choruses to the Lord and no one would hear me. So that is what I did as I worked and this had been going on for many days. On this one day as I walked back to the order desk all of a sudden I felt something whoosh past me and stand beside me brushing up against me. I couldn't visibly see who this was but I knew it had to be an angelic being because of what happened next. I got the feeling he interceded to protect me from unseen spiritual force that was being arrayed against me because the next thing I knew it seemed those enemy forces were being repelled away from where I was with great force. At the same time there was this pervasive heavenly aroma the exact same fragrance of the oil I had experienced on my hands and in the house where I had been studying months earlier. Then this heavenly presence briefly communicated with me not with words that anyone would hear but with thought telepathy concerning my future ministry.

Needless to say, I was so overwhelmed I was awestruck by the on-going experience. About ten feet away were some other workers and separating me from them was a high rack of parts they were using to fill orders for shipping. When I walked around to where they were, and when they took one look at me they knew something had happened, and then all of a sudden they detected the same fragrance that was filling the upper room and they were speechless.

I did my best to explain to them what had happened. Well the department leader hadn't been in the upper room when all this began happening and when he came upstairs the first thing he noticed was the heavenly aroma. At first he didn't want to believe our explanation so he went back downstairs looking for women that might have walked into the shop overwhelming everyone with their perfume. He didn't find any. This department leader was a faithful Catholic. A short time later he and his family began attending a Four Square church. That heavenly fragrance lasted for three days in the upper room before it finally dissipated.

We are given the free will to choose to serve Jesus or not serve Him. One can't afford to make the wrong choice! He returns as King in this generation!Have you chosen to be a part of His great kingdom?

Chapter Twenty Six
A Proper Acknowledgement

John 16.13 reads, "However, when He the Spirit of truth, has come, He will guide you into all truth; for He will not speak on His own authority, but whatever He hears He will speak; and He will tell you things to come."

How do we view the Holy Spirit? The Church is all <u>one</u> body in Christ yet differences in doctrine has caused separation between believers. If everyone understood Biblical doctrine the same way it would erase many of the misunderstandings that are presently known. With regard to the Holy Spirit a distinction needs to be made and clarified.

There is a difference between the Person of the Holy Spirit, and the gift of the Holy Spirit! Every true Christian needs to understand that when they become a born again Christian, at that moment, the Person of the Holy Spirit comes to dwell in them.

The Holy Spirit had not yet been given to Jesus' followers while He was with them, but He said, "And I will pray the Father, and He will give you another Helper, that He may abide with you forever - the Spirit of truth, whom the world cannot receive because it neither sees Him nor knows Him; but you know Him, for He dwells with you and will be <u>in you</u>" (John 14.16-17). So when did Jesus send the Holy Spirit to be in them? It was at Pentecost.

Some would say to me that the scripture there (in Acts 2.4) says they all spoke with other tongues. Yes, but bear with me and see the larger picture. There are two parts to their initial experience. First of all, it says "they were all filled with the Holy Spirit" which fulfilled what Jesus said, that the Holy Spirit would be in them. It is only after they were filled that we see the 120 speak in other tongues. So was it necessary for them to speak in other tongues? Yes and no.

You need to see what is happening here is the birth of the Church and it was Jesus' intention for the Church to be comprised of Jews and Gentiles. So the tongues were a sign to the Gentiles that the door had opened to them to be included with the Jewish people. Now it took a while for the disciples to get the message and this is why, for example, when Peter went to Cornelius' home (a Gentile) that when the Holy Spirit fell on them they also spoke in tongues (Acts 10.45-46) to convince Peter and those with him that God had accepted the Gentiles into the Church. It was not that tongues were required for one's salvation or even a required gift.

But this is how it should have been viewed, that the gift of speaking in other tongues was just that - one of the nine gifts of the Holy Spirit and not the Person of the Holy Spirit Himself. In fact, in Acts 10.45 and Acts 11.17 this spiritual experience was described as a gift from the Holy Spirit.

When the apostle Paul was addressing the Corinthian church and the exercising of the spiritual gifts he makes the following comment, "...all do not speak with tongues do they?" (1Corinthians 12.30).

This was an acknowledgment that not all believers had the gift of speaking in other tongues. Secondly, Paul further stated, "If anyone speaks in a tongue... if there is no interpreter he must keep silent in the church (1Corinthians 14.27-28). And then he goes on to say, "...let him speak to himself and to God." In other words, let your gift of tongues be your prayer language to God. Yes, Paul acknowledges the gift of tongues to be a legitimate spiritual gift but he also went on to say, "but earnestly desire the greater gifts" (1Cor.12.31).

So if someone thinks you haven't arrived until you receive the gift of tongues, I say you haven't arrived if you haven't received any of the greater gifts Paul said to seek after.

So why did I think it was important to include this last chapter? Because of the role the Holy Spirit plays in the translation of the saints. Ephesians 4.30 says, "And do not grieve the Holy Spirit of God, by whom you were sealed for the day of redemption."

Chapter Twenty Seven
The Destruction of Damascus

Isaiah chapter 17 has been a perplexing chapter to understand for Bible scholars, but now I believe it is beginning to reveal some of its mystery. I'll begin by quoting the first verse. "The burden against Damascus. Behold Damascus will cease from being a city and it will be a ruinous heap."

A few years after this prophecy it was conquered by the Assyrians in 732 B.C. But did that fulfill this prophecy? The answer is no. Because even after it was conquered it didn't cease from being a city. The fact that it is still a city let's us know this prophecy has an end time fulfillment yet to be realized.

We are given some clues as to when this will happen. It will be at a time when the cities of Aroer are also forsaken (v.2). The cities of Aroer were located east of the Dead Sea in what we call Jordan today but was in the Syrian domain when this was prophesied. The next clue is in verse four. "In that day it shall come to pass that the glory of Jacob will wane, and the fatness of his flesh grow lean."

So when does Israel's glory fade and grow dim? It is at the battle of Armageddon. Zechariah 13.8-9 makes it clear when this is. "And it shall come to pass in all the land, says the Lord, that two thirds in it shall be cut off and die, but one third shall be left in it: I will bring the one third through the fire, will refine them as silver is refined and test them as gold is tested. They will call on My name, and I will answer them. I will say this is My people; and each one will say, The Lord is my God." This accords with the words in Isaiah 17.7. "In that day a man will look to his Maker, and his eyes will have respect for the Holy One of Israel." In all honesty, Israel is not going to respect Jesus until He comes back and fights for Israel! This clinches the time period for Damascus' demise.

Now there is more going on here than just Damascus' demise. Isaiah 17.9 says, "In that day his strong cities will be as a forsaken bough and an uppermost branch, which they left because of the children of Israel; and there will be desolation." Why do these areas of Syria and Jordan become desolate at this time? It is to fulfill God's promise to Abraham (Genesis 15.18-21), Isaac (Genesis 26.4), and Jacob (Genesis 28.13-14) that these lands would become Israel's.

The last clue we will look at comes from Isaiah 17 verses 12 and 13. "Woe to the multitude of many people who make a noise like the roar of the seas, and to the rushing of nations that make a rushing like the rushing of mighty waters! The nations will rush like the rushing of many waters; but God will rebuke them and they will flee far away..." Now notice how this ties in with Revelation 19.15. "Now out of His mouth goes a sharp sword that with it He should strike the nations..." The person in this verse is, of course, referring to Jesus because in the next verse He is described as "King of Kings and Lord of Lords." At this point in Revelation chapter 19 Jesus is returning with the armies of heaven to end the battle of Armageddon.

So I conclude the fulfillment of this prophecy concerning Damascus is a few years off and that we don't need to expect it to happen right away.